The POWER Series
LAPD

Samuel M. Katz

Motorbooks International
Publishers & Wholesalers

First published in 1997 by Motorbooks International Publishers & Wholesalers, 729 Prospect Avenue, PO Box 1, Osceola, WI 54020-0001 USA

Motorbooks International books are also available at discounts in bulk quantity for industrial or sales-promotional use. For details write to Special Sales Manager at the Publisher's address

Library of Congress Cataloging-in-Publication Data

Katz, Samuel M.
    LAPD: including SWAT, undercover and patrol/
Samuel Katz.
        p. cm.
    Includes index.
    ISBN 0-7603-0230-8 (pbk. : alk. paper)
    1. Los Angeles (Calif.). Police Dept.--History.
    2. Police- Angeles--Special weapons and tactics units--History. I. Title.
    HV8148.L55K38   1997
    363.2'097794'94--dc21   97-9046

Front cover: SWAT officers fire a Starflash munition through the bathroom window of a targeted narcotics location in Southeast Division's notorious Nickerson Gardens.

Frontispiece: The LAPD patch—a badge of honor for the officers and a symbol of concern for criminals.

Title page: During rescue training in breaching a barricaded location, SWAT officers deploy an explosive charge to burst through a front door of a training field's "killing house." Courtesy: Sergeant A.R. Preciado

Back cover: Sergeant Kerchenske points to El Salvadoran gang graffiti that marks a back alley where a young mother was car-jacked and brutally raped.

Edited by Mike Haenggi
Designed by Katie Finney

Printed in Hong Kong through World Print, Ltd.

CONTENTS

ACKNOWLEDGMENTS

My first walk inside a Los Angeles Police Department station house came one "very chilly" February morning when I left the chaotic bustle of LAX for the windswept shores of Pacific Area. The station, a modern brick square building surrounded by palm trees and a parking lot full of neatly washed black-and-white patrol cars, was everything police stations in New York City weren't—it was clean, organized, and the definition of calm. As I walked to the front desk, carrying my suitcase and camera bag, a motorcycle cop, wearing a neatly pressed uniform and a white helmet shined to a glowing reflection, walked up to me and simply helped me with my bags. At the front desk, a young female "boots," as P-I probationary officers are called, stood her post answering a telephone that seemed never to stop ringing. "Los Angeles Police Department, Pacific Area, how may I serve you?" she said, as the caller on the other end complained of a foul odor coming from a car abandoned in her driveway. "Don't worry, Ma'am," the probie replied "I'll have a patrol car respond immediately. Have a nice day." Have a nice day? What kind of police station was this? Where was the peeling paint? Leaking water-pipes? Where was the profanity? Where was the picture of the Three Stooges in police uniforms hanging on the wall above the desk sergeant's roll call clipboard?

This certainly didn't look like a precinct back home!

So what is a born-and-bred New Yorker doing writing a book about a police department on the other side of the country? Good question. I must admit that only a few years ago, my knowledge of the Los Angeles Police Department was restricted to headlines, rumors, and a potpourri of images embedded in my mind from too many hours in front of the TV watching bad cop shows set in Los Angeles. My expertise was on the Israel Defense Forces and counter-terrorism, nothing even remotely connected to Los Angeles, nor to American law enforcement for that matter. Then, several years ago, I began writing about the NYPD and its Emergency Service Unit, and I was hooked. I became a buff. My admiration and respect for cops simply became the focus of my work, and I found myself in the very enviable position of making a living writing about people whom I respected and admired—those whose courage and dedication amazed me. Then, in 1994, I was commissioned to write an encyclopedia examining counter-terrorist units from around the world—both military and police—and my professional interests left the five boroughs of New York City and headed west. I made contact with the Los Angeles Police Department's elite SWAT Platoon. Having talked to SEALs and operators from the U.S. Army's 1st SFOD-Delta in the course of my work, I had always heard that LAPD SWAT was something of a beacon in the art of tactical professionalism—a trendsetter that was emulated throughout this country and even the world.

Luck is a tremendous tool in a writer's repertoire, and in beginning my research into the LAPD and its SWAT unit, I was incredibly fortunate to have been hooked in with Sergeant Al R. Preciado, the unit's senior sergeant who has probably forgotten more about SWAT work than most unit commanders will ever know. Sergeant Preciado, known as 20-David in the unit's vernacular, opened my eyes to a unit that had revolutionized police tactical deployment in this country, personified by professionalism and dedication. If I had to have a teacher in learning about the LAPD, Sergeant Al Preciado was its Rhodes Scholar. His stories and detailed knowledge of the A-to-Zs of SWAT work were an inspiration to me, sparking my interest in the LAPD. When I wrote a full-length illustrated book on the NYPD Emergency Service Unit in 1995, and happily learned that a book that was pro-police could find an audience, I right away knew what department I would focus on next. I called Sergeant Preciado, and he kindly agreed to serve as my "Rabbi" in the department. The rest is history.

This book would never have happened without Sergeant Preciado, and I owe him a debt I can never hope to repay. From being his personal guest at the 1996 annual SWAT dinner, to watching him in action on an obstacle course, to watching him on a job "hot and heavy," while serving a search warrant in the mean stretches of Los Angeles, he generously availed himself as my guide and teacher. Watching Sergeant Preciado on an obstacle course was an inspiration. Having him as a friend and guide in the LAPD was of incredible fortune to me. Sergeant Preciado is a walking encyclopedia and an operator who can outrun, out-shoot, and out-climb men half his age. Having him on the job in Los Angeles is a great asset to the residents of the City of Angels.

Sergeant Al Preciado, LAPD SWAT, discusses a training schedule with his officers.

Sergeant Preciado is truly a unique individual of unquestioned skill and experience, but he is not alone in the ranks of the department and his unit. I would like to offer a special word of thanks to Lieutenant Tom Runyen, the platoon commander, who was incredibly kind and supportive to "this stranger" from back East, and who made me a feel at home in the unit. During training and during actual operations, Lieutenant Runyen was a guide and a teacher, and, as a former Marine, a shining example to the officers in his command. I would like to offer a special word of thanks to Sergeant Andy Lamprey for his kindness and assistance, and to the commander of Metropolitan Division, Captain Bud Lewallen, for his support and assistance.

This book would also not have been possible without the support of Commander Tim McBride, and my great pillars of support in the Press Relations Office—Officer Helen Lloyd, and the OIC (officer in charge), Lieutenant Anthony Alba. I would also like to offer a very special word of thanks to Lieutenant John Dunkin, the commanding officer of South Bureau Homicide. A former paratrooper and commander of the Press Relations Office, Lieutenant Dunkin took a great deal of time out of his busy schedule to give me an impromptu course in the art of detective work, police management, and the mental portrait of the gang-bangers and wanton killers that plague Los Angeles. I would also like to offer a special word of thanks—and best wishes upon his retirement—to Sergeant John Paige of Newton CRASH. Sergeant Paige is a true cop's cop—a supervisor and the first through the door, a man with more analytical abilities behind the squint of an eye when looking at a "knucklehead's" excuses than a mountain of paperwork from a crime-lab think tank. Sergeant Paige taught me a lot about police work in Los Angeles. He taught me about what it takes to fight gangs and narcotics, and he taught me a hell of a lot about courage and character.

I spent a lot of time with many different units and shifts in the department, and space precludes me from thanking them all. I would like to thank Lieutenant Ron McCall and Sergeant Donn Yarnall of the K-9 unit for their time and assistance; I would like to thank Sergeant Joe Klorman and Sergeant Steve Vinson of Hollywood Area; Sergeant Bill Frio of Pacific Area; Sergeant Leo Kerchenske, Southeast Area SPU; Detective Brent Josephson, South Bureau Homicide; Lieutenant Earl Paysinger, Mounted Unit; Daniel Esgro, police reservist with SWAT; Sergeant Don Schwartzer, Metro Division; and Richard E. Kalk, the President of the Los Angeles Police Historical Society.

Finally, I would like to offer a special word of thanks to my agent, Al Zuckerman, for his inspiration, invaluable assistance, and representation.

Police work is a lot like breathing—it is something that must happen all the time for life as we know it to continue. Because there are cops on the beat, detectives pounding the pavement, K-9 "officers" racing through a hillside, and police chopper pilots airborne twenty-four hours a day, it is impossible, in a book of this format (or any other format) and size to provide a complete depiction of what a police department has done for the past 150 years, never mind what it does on a day-to-day basis. As a result, I have attempted to provide a brief illustrated glimpse of perhaps this nation's finest police department at work, protecting and serving the citizens of the city of Los Angeles.

This book is dedicated to the men and women of the Los Angeles Police Department. Through all the hardships and dangers they endure, through the media scrutiny and natural disasters, they have proven time after time that they are second to none.

Samuel M. Katz

INTRODUCTION

This is the city. Los Angeles, California.

For generations, the scratchy voice of Jack Webb introducing a radio and then television audience to the world of the Los Angeles Police Department was a glimpse into a place that few knew of and even fewer understood. The series "Dragnet," in both its radio and television formats, might appear tame, even Pollyannaish, by today's level of tolerance of blood and gore, but the weekly episodes were slices of life taken directly from the files of the Los Angeles Police Department. The show wasn't meant to depict bloodshed and fear, nor was it designed to examine to social reasons behind crime in the City of Angels. It was meant as a testament to the professionalism and almost rigid code of behavior and duty present in the heart and soul of every Los Angeles cop. It was a code that was maintained to conviction in the 1940s and 1950s, it was held with religious fervor in the 1960s, and it remains intact to this day.

Los Angeles is a city that needs, for lack of a better word, a different type of police officer because it is a city in the United States, and the world for that matter.

> *"The City of Los Angeles has the most professional police officers in the world"*
> —A Vatican official following Pope John Paul II's visit to Los Angeles in September 1987.

Less a patchwork of neighborhoods, boroughs, and eastside and westside sections, Los Angeles is a maze of off-ramps and freeways, boulevards and avenues, cut across by the Hollywood hills, the Valley, and the Pacific Ocean. At 466 square miles, the city of Los Angeles is the most spread-out city in the world. With its resident population of over 3.59 million, and another three or four million people coming in from the surrounding counties every day, Los Angeles is a law enforcement micro-manager's worst nightmare. It is a city carved jaggedly into neat and obtrusive rectangular boundaries, criss-crossing areas under the control of varying departments and jurisdictions—including the County Sheriff's Office, the Beverly Hills Police Department, the Long Beach Police Department, and the California Highway Patrol. Los Angeles has also been home to some of the most spectacular and brutal crimes in American law enforcement history—from the Black Dahlia case of the 1940s, to the 1966 Watts Riots, to the Manson Family and the horrendous Tate and Labianca killings, to the Night Stalker, Rodney King, and O.J. Simpson. For a city and a police department trying valiantly to keep its finger in the dike and maintain law and order, and constantly battling the media and the elements (earthquakes and fires), Los Angeles is a city continually on the brink.

Making law enforcement in Los Angeles all the more remarkable is the fact that the LAPD boasts fewer than 9,200 officers on the force—including the current Chief of Police all the way down to the recruit doing 20 push-ups at the academy. It made more arrests, over a larger land mass, per capita than any other police force in the world—the NYPD, for example, deploys 89 officers per square mile, while the LAPD deploys only 15. When considering the fact that New York City, with a land mass half that of Los Angeles and a population only slightly larger, boasts a police department with nearly 40,000 officers, one can see why the LAPD has developed a professional ethic like no other force in the country—not because of any divine inspiration, but because it has had to in order to survive. Throughout its history, the LAPD has always been damned if it does, and dead if it doesn't. Damned, it was always argued, was a lot better than dead. For years, the LAPD employed a pro-active, para-military-like approach to policing that was both effective and, to many, controversial.

Survival has always been a matter of dubious distinction in Los Angeles, a metropolis built around a frontier town in America's romantic and violent west. The Spanish first visited the plush and mountainous landscape in 1769 and established a town there in 1781. The area remained in Spanish and later Mexican control until 1846, when it was captured from Mexico and four years later incorporated into the United States. Soon after California's inclusion into the union, a Gold Rush economy spurned expansion by the railroads, establishing Los Angeles as a hub of the American West. However, with this boom it also became the crime capital of the West. Los Angeles circa 1850 was a town where the strongest survived, one who was slow on a trigger finger ended up in a pine box. A mosaic of cultures, languages, colors, and religions attempted to live together in peace and harmony. If Los Angeles in the 1850s need-

ed anything, it was a police department—the city was literally a talent-pool of every bandit, gunslinger, killer, con-artist, rustler, and extortionist known in the West. Benjamin D. Wilson, the second mayor of Los Angeles, appointed the city's "first" peace officer in 1851—a no-nonsense lawman named Samuel Whiting. Whiting was tasked with keeping law and order in a city of just about 1,610 souls. Sharing Whiting's duties were his deputies and the office of the Los Angeles County Sheriff. Unofficially, he also received help from vigilante committees made of local residents exacting their own brand of frontier justice. There were no televised court proceedings in those early days of Los Angeles, no dream team of lawyers, and no winning of the public's hearts and minds. Horse thieves and cattle rustlers were routinely shot at dawn.

City Marshal Whiting and his successors were overwhelmed by the crime in their midst, and tempted by the corruption that was the soul and everyday currency of a city in its infant stages. In 1853, following the murder of a City Marshal, the Los Angeles Mounted Rangers were formed. Under the command of Dr. Alexander W. Hope, Rangers wore ribbon badges on their hide-skin tunics. On them the following words were imprinted in Spanish and English: "City Police, Authorized by the Council of Los Angeles." The Rangers were responsible for the pursuit and death in Tejon Pass of the notorious bandit Joaqin Murrieta, and other criminals who committed murders, robberies, and rapes without remorse and let-up.

County Sheriff James Barton took office in 1851. He was killed by outlaws six years later, an event that-spurred a rare but massive roundup of criminals. Of the 52 suspects arrested, 11 were summarily executed. The prisoner specifically charged with Barton's murder was later removed from jail by vigilantes and hanged. Barton's successor, Sheriff William C. Getman, was murdered by a demented suspect who, in turn, was killed in a subsequent shootout with heavily armed Mexican bandits.

Yet the modern LAPD of today, the one equipped with ASTRO radios and in-car computerized MDTs

(Mobile Digital Terminals), can truly trace back their departmental history to 1869 when the city reached deep into its vault and authorized the salaries for six full-time police officers. Armed with side arms and batons, the six peace officers worked in two shifts and attempted to provide a measure of law and order to the ever-growing legions of individuals flocking to the city. The six officers soon grew into dozens as Los Angeles became a more volatile and dangerous frontier town. There were almost as many saloons, brothels, and opium dens in the town as there were residents. Lawlessness was pervasive, as were wanton acts of robbery and murder. The easiest targets of the day were Chinese laborers. They were routinely robbed, lynched, and beaten. They were often murdered in cold blood.

The salaries for the city's first peace officers came from collected fees and fines. Warren was destined to die of gunshot wounds sustained in a dispute with one of his officers in 1870. Also in 1870, the City Counsel appointed three of its members to form the first Board of Police Commissioners, examining the role and operations of the city's law enforcement personnel.

From 1870 to the early 1900s, the department grew from a dozen cops, armed with .45 caliber revolvers and 45-70 rifles, into a force of over 100 officers including detectives, traffic enforcement, and patrol vehicles. Horses and buggies replaced by the automobile responded to thousands of calls a year.

From 1900 to the late 1940s, the city and the department grew by leaps and bounds. The LAPD was renown nationwide for its innovative and trend-setting style. It was the first department in the nation to hire a female officer, the first department to hire a black officer, the first department to hire a Hispanic officer, the first department to hire an Asian officer, and it was the first department to have a Jewish Chief of Police. With Los Angeles becoming the car capital of the world, the department became the nation's leading traffic enforcement force and in 1913 it created its "speed squad," the forerunner of today's motorcycle cop. By the dawn of

The bust of Chief William H. Parker at LAPD HQ in Parker Center in downtown Los Angeles.

the depression, the city's endless opportunities and far-reaching film industry brought lots of money to southern California and that brought corruption—corruption which, inevitably, reached the ranks of the LAPD. The "C" word would hang over the LAPD for many years. The man who brought the LAPD out of its dark period and really into the modern age was Chief James

A throwback to the old days of Dragnet—an LAPD detective combs through his files at Bunco-Forgery Section located at LAPD HQ in Parker Center.

Edgar Davis, a national pistol champion who, according to one historian, "took s**t from no one."

Yet the true turning point in the history of the modern Los Angeles Police Department came in August 1950 when a veteran LAPD commander with a stellar war record took the helm of a leaderless force rocked by scandal and corruption. That man was Chief William H. Parker, and American law enforcement was never the same. Chief Parker brought with him a military-like code of conduct when he assumed command of the department, and he expected his officers to be honest, professional, disciplined, cour-

teous, and role models for the rest of the citizens of Los Angeles. Chief Parker was the law—pure and simple. He was a fair man, but strict beyond the definition of the word. His tolerance for shenanigans and some of the liberties officers had taken under previous administrations was zero. You did your job on the force because you believe it to be a sanctimonious and honored profession—not to get by or to get rich. An officer that drove to police headquarters in a car that even smelled new was immediately placed under Internal Affairs scrutiny. Uniforms had to be pressed and ironed. Creases in an officer's trousers had to be sharp and badges had to be polished to a sparkling shine. If Chief Parker found an officer displaying a sloppy appearance, that officer would have wished to have been assigned a foot post in hell, because it was nothing compared to the misery of being on the chief's s**t list. Yet officers who performed their duties honestly, professionally, and with vigor knew that the man at the top would always be there to back them up. His famous quote, "With all the fiber in his being he would see to it that the crooked rats who would turn the City of Angels to the City of Diablos will not do so, and that the LAPD would work for the community, not rule it" (Joe Domanick, *To Protect and To Serve: The LAPD's Century of War In The City Of Dreams* [New York: Pocket Books, 1995], 103).

Chief Parker brought military discipline to the ranks in the department, and he brought law and order to the streets. He initiated pro-active policing among the men and women of the department. They were forceful, visible, omnipresent, and intimidated by nothing. So successful was Chief Parker in his duties, so respected was he by the men and women in the department, that many joked the only way he'd leave police headquarters was at the ripe old age of 100. But America in the 1960s was a changing landscape of turmoil and racial tension, and Los Angeles would not be spared the violence. There

A suspect is brought into custody in northern Los Angeles, circa 1955. *LAPD Press Relations Office*

Before the days of mobile display terminals, two-way radios, and cruise control, an LAPD black-and-white prepares to go out on patrol. *LAPD Press Relations Office*

were many in the black community who believed the LAPD to be a racist force and one that often targeted the minorities with brutal beatings and harsh and disrespectful treatment. In August 1965, riots erupted in the Watts ghetto, in South Central Los Angeles, following the arrest of a black motorist by a white police officer. The reasons behind the outburst of violence were irrelevant, it could have—and some say would have—been caused by a million and one incidents bound to happen on the city streets in the heat and passion of a summer of national turmoil. The results, however, were deadly. Rioters set fire to their own community, shops were looted, homes destroyed, and dozens of lives lost—including several police officers cut down in cold blood by sniper fire. It was a full-scale war fought on a small patch of urban Los Angeles and it rocked the city to its core. Watts and South Central never recovered from the 1966 riots—to this day the remnants of the urban chaos are evident throughout the inner city. Chief Parker never recovered from the riots, either. Taken aback by the civil unrest under his watch, he was never the same man after the riots. He died a year later.

The LAPD has for years—in both the pre and post riot years—been known as the nation's most professional force. In fact, if the LAPD can be called anything, it is the nation's true innovator in modern police work, modern police tactics, and effective police strategies. The LAPD's innovative character comes more out of practicality than anything else. It has, for nearly 100 years, had to deploy wit and guile in order to maintain law and order with such a small department. Being centered in the movie-production capital of the world, the LAPD, with television shows like Dragnet and Adam-12, became the first municipal police department to effectively and ambitiously market itself. It also became a pioneer in the use of motorcycle cops, it was the first department, with the "formal" creation of the SWAT Platoon in 1971, to embrace the concept of creating a tactically elite para-military like unit tasked with high-risk warrants, counter-sniper duty, and hostage-rescue. The Los Angeles Police Department was also the country's pioneer in the deployment of helicopters—not only

The man who was the father of the modern LAPD—Chief William Parker. *LAPD Press Relations Office*

for aerial patrolling and traffic reports, but to aggressively and tactically support patrol officers in the field. The department was among the nation's first in using its K-9 units in a tactical mode, and was the first department to pro-actively provide its officers with stress-management counseling.

In March 1978, the Los Angeles Police Department would enjoy yet another turning point, when Daryl Gates, a fire-branding officer who had, at one time, been Chief Parker's driver, was named Chief of Police. Chief Gates was a controversial figure in the City of Angels for his unique, and often aggressive, anti-crime strategies and his unforgiving approach toward criminals. Chief Gates was committed to the men and women who served under him and the bond between Gates and the officers in the department remains infrangible even to this day; many in the department, veteran cops with as much as

Parker Center—the Los Angeles Police Department's headquarters. *LAPD Press Relations Office*

twenty-five years on the job, still consider Gates to be the only chief the department has truly ever known.

Chief Gates was a hand's-on commander. He enjoyed spending time with the SWAT on raids, and he personally commanded drug busts—he even obtained for the department a V-100 armored car fitted with a fourteen-foot-long battering ram designed to break through the walls of crack dens. The officers adored "the chief" but he became an easy target for his detractors and the media. Los Angeles is a media capital, where the bizarre, the unjust, the blown-out-of-proportion is all camera feed to newscasts; Gates was on the local news more than anyone else. His penchant for calling drug dealers the Viet Cong, plus his presence on high-media police operations, his silver chief stars prominently displayed, ruffled many feathers in the city's governing bodies, especially Mayor Tom Bradley. Both Bradley and Gates had graduated from the Los Angeles Police Academy in the 1940s, though Bradley had resigned from the force in the early 1960s mainly, it has been reported, because of the department's rigid bosses and unyielding attitudes. Under Gates, though, from the department's superb handling of the 1984 Summer Olympics in Los Angeles to the cre-

ation of CRASH units in the war against gangs, the department moved light years ahead in its campaign to keep Los Angeles a safe and livable city.

Yet whatever advances the department makes, the city's explosive nature, something akin to the power of the ever-present threat of earthquakes, always rocks the city and the department to the core. The March 1991 beating of Rodney L. King, a drunk motorist racing through the city streets at nearly 100 mph, began as a California Highway Patrol car-stop-gone-bad and eventually became a videotaped testimony of what to many was endemic of a racist, brutal, and neo-Nazi- like mentality of the LAPD. The four officers caught on camera in the beating were eventually brought to trial, but when they were acquitted on April 29, 1992, their vindication became a causus belli for a public insurrection. On the corner of Florence and Normandie, in the confines of the notorious 77th Street Area, the 1992 riots began with the savage beating of white truck driver Reginald Denny. Soon, much of Los Angeles was engulfed in wanton savagery and an unbridled release of violent aggression. In police stations throughout the city, officers fetched their riot gear and pumped their shotguns, but there was little they could do. At the onset of the crisis, at a critical juncture in the city's and department's history, decisive command was absent. Several hours of police indecisiveness and the public scrutiny fueled by the media's desire to cover a story rather than the truth permitted chaos to engulf much of South Central Los Angeles. The department could not pro-actively stop looters and snipers starting fires and then picking off LAFD personnel one-by-one, since that would justify the citizens' uprising, as many in the media referred to the "opportunity to murder and steal." With over 50 dead and countless more wounded, and property damage in the hundreds of millions of dollars, the National Guard was summoned to the city of angels. Men in BDUs armed with M-16 assault rifles patrolled Watts and much of the city. The riots, once again, turned Los Angeles into the Wild West. With Washington and the world watching, the end of an era would come to the Los Angeles Police Department. A presidential-appointed commission, headed by soon-to-be Secretary of State Warren Christopher, was tasked with redesigning the department.

One of the major recommendations of the Christopher Commission was that the city be empowered to limit the term of a police chief or fire him. Other recommendations included an increased hiring of blacks, females, and Asians, and that officers be taught sensitivity awareness in their dealings with the public. Daryl Gates, chief of police for fourteen years and on the job for over forty, was forced to resign. He was replaced by Willie Williams, the former police chief of Philadelphia and the first African-American to lead the LAPD. He was also its second chief selected from outside the department.

Finally, and still ongoing, there was the case of O.J. Simpson and the murders of Nicole Brown Simpson and Ron Goldman. But what should have been the arrest and trial of a man charged with a double homicide instead became a soap-box for LAPD bashing—from the racist sentiments of a detective to the integrity of the department's crime lab—televised to a global audience. Like many big cases in which it finds itself embroiled, the LAPD could not win in the O.J. Simpson ordeal—if he was found guilty, his lawyers hinted in the obtuse language of the eye-squint and sound-byte, another riot would erupt. When he was found innocent by a jury many believed to have reviewed the case along racial lines, the department was rocked by self-doubt and a morale crisis the likes of which had never been seen before in the department's history.

Today the department is attempting to redefine its character, rethink its role, and, following nearly 100 years of by-the-book pro-active policing, embrace the concept of community policing.

Like the city it serves, a metropolis always in search of the newest trend, the LAPD is a force constantly reinventing itself, under intense—and often unfair—scrutiny, and a department that is caught in a cyclic Catch-22 of being damned if it does, and screwed if it doesn't. The fact that the department is able to police at all given the intense political roadblocks and environmental challenges it faces is by itself a statement of professional prowess. The fact that it can police the city with such skill, determination, and innovation is a testament to the men and women who attend roll call each morning, gear up, and patrol the city's streets with motivation and zeal. For it is they who have made the department a role model for police agencies in the United States and the entire world.

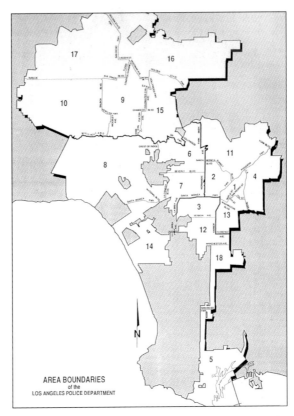

AREA BOUNDARIES
of the
LOS ANGELES POLICE DEPARTMENT

(1) Central; (2) Rampart; (3) Southwest; (4) Hollenbeck; (5) Harbor; (6) Hollywood; (7) Wilshire; (8) West Los Angeles; (9) Van Nuys; (10) West Valley; (11) Northeast; (12) 77th Street; (13) Newton; (14) Pacific; (15) North Hollywood; (16) Foothill; (17) Devonshire; (18) Southeast. *LAPD Press Relations Office*

CHAPTER ONE

THE ACADEMY
The Making of LA's Finest

It is nearly midnight on a balmy September night, and the roar of the crowd emanates from the canyon at Chavez Ravine with thunderous might. The Los Angeles Dodgers, trying to inch their way toward a playoff berth, are at bat in the bottom of the ninth, and the crowd, what's left of it, is looking for another miracle come-from-behind win. Within earshot of Dodgers Stadium, at the eastern entrance to Elysian Park, a group of men and women are also searching for a miracle. They have been up for eighteen hours and their royal blue police-department-issue sweatsuits are soaked with perspiration and grime. They have just completed a two-mile run, and hope that the instructor will provide them with at least a respite from push-ups and sit-ups before they head back to the books and yet another day of instruction.

Nobody ever said it would be easy to become one of LA's finest!

The Los Angeles Police Academy is undoubtedly the world's most famous police instructional facility in the world—after all, it has been used as a backdrop by more bad police TV shows than any other location in the city other than the Hollywood sign. The facility looks more like a country club than a law enforcement academy, but any thoughts of having martinis by the pool and soaking in the California sun are interrupted by the crackling of gunfire and the barks of the instructors. On the parade ground, an instructor is running a class around the track at an unforgiving pace, while nearby, a firearms instructor is going through the stripping of a Remington 12-gauge shotgun. In another classroom, officers are taught the fine art of subduing a suspect with a baton, while elsewhere officer-hopefuls are taught the A-to-Zs of "probable cause." The setting of the Police Academy might be picturesque, but the business taught there is deadly serious.

Of all the jobs in American law enforcement, becoming an officer in the Los Angeles Police Department might not be one of the highest paying in the country (certainly not in the state), but it is the most prestigious. It attracts people from all around the city, the county, the state, the region, the country, and even the entire world. "The LAPD is the real world," claims John, a recently discharged paratrooper sergeant from the 82nd Airborne who is taking his preliminary examinations at the academy in the hope of being accepted into a class. "I don't care what people say about a police career and a civil-ser-

A greeting that says it all—a reminder to all LAPD recruits that they are soon to become among the finest law enforcement officers in the world.

A mural at the LAPD Police Academy running track meant to provide confidence, momentum, and staying power to recruits of each passing class.

vice job being the 'white man's welfare,' if you want to learn about law enforcement this is the place to learn and this city is the place to work." John's accent, Kentucky bluegrass, is definitely not California. Indeed, many of those who try out for the LAPD are "foreigners" to the city, migrants from such exotic places as Lubbock, Texas; Cleveland, Ohio; Honolulu, Hawaii; and even New York City. There is even a sergeant on the force who used to be a bobby in the London Metropolitan Police. Like many who enter the academy, they come to Los Angeles first on a visit, and then find the sunshine, mobility, and opportunities a reason for staying.

Because it is, relatively speaking, such a small force, the LAPD is also extremely selective, and competition for slots in the "next class" is fierce. Entry into the department, it should be added, is purely by merit. No hooks, connections, or intervening "rabbis." It is one of the fairest approaches to taking people on the job that exists in law enforcement today in the United States. Yet each time the LAPD hires, the throng of applicants and the subsequent competition guarantee two things—the department gets to pick and hire the best individuals suited for police work, and that a lot of people will be heading home very disappointed.

The department realizes that many who sign up for a class have a somewhat "less-than-accurate" view of the department—from what the department demands from its personnel to what the job is actually like. These wannabes have, in many cases, had their impression of the department forged by years of watching television and movies, and the department tries as best as possible to spell out the job preview to every applicant before he or she enters through the academy's gates. "We want the officers to want the job not because of the glamour or the firearm," claims an instructor who has seen his share of brilliant pupils, as well as those who were bounced out in a flash-of-an-eye, "but rather because the job, in all aspects, appeals to that individual."

Before an applicant signs on for the test, they are asked to read a small pamphlet in which the job, in all its glory and occasional boredom, is spelled out. This official job preview, with its mandated requirements, includes:

- Police Officers are required to fill out many different forms, logs, and reports. Correspondingly, Police Officers must write legibly and clearly and have a good working knowledge of English grammar, sentence structure, vocabulary, and spelling. Police Officers must be concise, descriptive, and thorough in all written documents.
- Police Officers constantly communicate with members of the community. It is crucial to initi-

"The Academy" as it's known in the LAPD vernacular, becomes home to the recruits during their training, and a source of pride after they graduate.

ate contact with members of the community to better understand the needs and problems of a particular area. Police Officers must possess excellent communication and interpersonal skills to interact with the public on a daily basis. Police Officers also must interview and obtain information from victims and witnesses of crimes in a manner appropriate to the situation and culture of the people involved.

• Police Officers meet with and make presentations to groups of residents and/or business people from various neighborhoods regarding local crime, traffic, and related problems.

• Police Officers may be required to work the front desk at a police station. This involves numerous activities including answering phone calls from the public, taking reports, explaining the law and LAPD policies, listening and responding to complaints about police service, and handling complaints from citizens who walk into the station.

• Police Officers must testify accurately and credibly in court regarding arrests, reports taken, evidence recovered, and victims' statements.

• Police Officers must employ excellent listening skills, in person and on the telephone.

21

During an outdoor lunch, two recruits gulp down a quick meal before returning to the firing range for some handgun proficiency training.

Officers must listen closely to what is being said and retain that information, identifying needs and emotions being expressed and demonstrating interest and involvement.

• Police Officers deal with all segments of society. Some members of the general public may have hostile feelings toward Police Officers and may express their hostility to the Officer in words or actions. A Police Officer must always behave professionally in the face of provocation.

• Police Officers must evaluate situations, determine whether a crime has taken place, and make an independent decision as to what action

is appropriate. In doing so, the Officer must simultaneously consider numerous factors, recognize patterns, and develop theories based on available information and evidence.

• Police Officers must attend daily roll call meeting, as vital information is given about planned activities, suspects, or suspicious activities, and crimes in their area. Officers must organize this information for use during their shift. Officers must plan and complete their activities and paperwork in a timely and efficient manner.

• Police Officers must pay attention to detail, noticing minute elements or components of a

Their Berettas still void of live ammunition, a group of classmates discuss their curriculum and what awaits them on a test concerning non-lethal force.

particular person or crime scene. Officers must also be able to visualize and recall an event after the fact in order to construct documentation of the event, possibly for future court testimony. Officers also recognize and gather evidence at the scene of a crime, and they are responsible for the safe storage and transportation of this evidence.

• Police Officers are required to learn and memorize large quantities of complex and detailed material, including Penal Codes; legal terms; LAPD procedures and policies; Health and Safety Codes; Laws of Arrest; Search and Seizure Law; Laws of Evidence; etc.

• Police Officers must be able to operate a computerized Mobile Digital Terminal (MDT). Officers must use the keyboard and special function keys using LAPD call codes and computer language to access the various types of information needed. Officers also use the MDT to receive assigned coded calls and communications from other units. Officers must be able to accurately initiate and respond to clear, precise communications over the MDT.

• Police Officers must use problem solving and reasoning skills in order to initiate innova-

Part of the academy obstacle course—up-and-down obstacles and twisting mountain paths have broken a countless number of LAPD hopefuls.

to eight hours; physically subduing, detaining, and arresting combative suspects; physically searching suspects; rescuing civilians by dragging and carrying aided cases to safety; performing CPR and first-aid procedures; and serving high-risk arrest and search warrants.

• Police Officers must be able to work in all parts of the city limits and deal with all of the city's inhabitants, under a gamut of conditions and environments. Officers may be required to search and touch suspects who are dirty, neglected, injured, and bleeding. Some of the individuals could have potentially life-threatening infectious diseases, such as tuberculosis and AIDS. Police officers are also required to remain open-minded, unbiased, and sensitive to a person's religion, race, and sexual persuasion.

• Once probable cause has been established, the officer must detain and/or arrest suspects and take them into custody. This might involve the use of LAPD-approved techniques of restraint, including control holds, batons, guns, and handcuffs to physically subdue suspects.

tive solutions to difficult and unique problems which are faced while on duty.

• Police Officers must be mediators, resolving conflicts such as business, neighborly, family, and traffic-related disputes—all that have the potential of escalating into crimes, felonies, and violent outbursts.

• Police Officers must monitor and control crowds at locations where better judgment and emotions are not always calm and civil.

• Police Officers must exhibit leadership by taking command and control of developing situations, delegating tasks, and serving as examples.

• Police Officers must use their taught and inherent interpersonal skills to calm distraught persons, subdue angry or combative individuals, and to convince uncooperative individuals that "cooperation" is an advised course of behavior.

• Police work involves physical exertion and endurance, and can include: pursuing suspects on vehicle or on foot; walking a foot patrol for up

The most important aspect that the department tries to instill in an individual hoping to be accepted into the department is that once he/she is accepted into the academy, once the uniform is on and the badge securely fastened (and properly polished), that the officer is a representative of the city of Los Angeles and, as a result, is a symbol of stability, trust, honesty, and morality to the citizens he/she serve.

New officer candidates to the LAPD must, of course, bear the results of many painful controversies and crisis that the department has been forced to endure over the past quarter century, from Rodney King to O.J., from Watts to the war against the Bloods and Crips. Anyone still interested in a job with the Los Angeles Police Department, however, and still confident enough in his/her abilities to protect and to serve the citizens of Los Angeles, must meet the following requirements:

• An applicant must be at least twenty-one years old.
• An applicant must be a United States High

24

Classroom study—an essential part of the curriculum at the LAPD academy. "You'll need the classroom," claims an instructor to his class, "before we can turn you loose and let you learn on the streets."

School Graduate, or a G.E.D. equivalent from a United States institution. A two- or four-year college degree from an accredited college or university, or prior law enforcement employment, enables a higher start-up salary.

• Applicants need not be U.S. citizens when seeking employment, though noncitizens must have begun the process for citizenship prior to submitting the application.

• An applicant must have a clean record—nobody with a prior felony convictions or any misdemeanor conviction that would preclude the legal carrying of a firearm can apply. There must also be no history of criminal or improper conduct, poor employment or a poor military record, or poor driving record (a California driving license is required) which may affect one's suitability for law enforcement work.

• In physical terms, an applicant's distance visual acuity must be no worse than 20/40 uncorrected. Applicants must have normal functional color vision.

• Applicants must be at least five feet tall, with an appropriate body fat percentage (no more than 22 percent for men and 30 percent for women).

ABOVE AND BELOW: At the academy's firing range, detectives practice before having to qualify. Being firearms proficient becomes an LAPD must—from day one at the academy to retirement.

If an LAPD officer-wannabe meets all those criteria, he/she must then pass a seven-step selection process many consider to be the toughest in the nation. The selection includes a written test, interview, medical examination, written psychological test, an extensive background investigation, physical abilities test, and a psychological interview. The qualifying written test consists of two parts: A multiple-choice test designed to measure reading comprehension and English usage, and an essay designed to measure candidates' written communication skills. Both tests are "pass-fail." The interview, the next step up the ladder, lasts approximately twenty minutes and is 100 percent of the final score in the Police Officer examination. Interview boards usually consist of a sworn member of the

Police Department, usually a supervising Sergeant or Detective, and a City Personnel Department representative. Questions asked focus on problem-solving abilities, respect for diversity, community service orientation, role adaptability, and personal accomplishments. Passing the interview requires a minimum score of 70 percent. One applicant, upon taking the interview, couldn't believe how closely the set-up reminded him of an episode of Dragnet he had watched on late-night TV weeks before taking the test. "You'd think that Sergeant Joe Friday and Officer Gannon were giving me the test, and you know the questions were almost similar!"

Once the applicant passes the written and interview portions of their process, he or she must endure what to many is their last test and final contact with the LAPD (unless they are later arrested, of course): the medical examination/written psychological test. Both tests are administered on the same day at the same location and take nearly six hours to complete. Applicants must bring a completed medical history, though a *complete* physical examination (the political correctness of this book precludes any further elaboration) is administered by departmental doctors. Doctors aren't looking for any hidden impairments, or mysterious black shadows on X-rays, but rather are in search of conditions that would restrict an applicant's ability to safely do police work. The written psychological test—considered the "great weeder out"—consists of several personality and life-history questionnaires and is evaluated by a team of staff psychologists. Anyone hoping for a spot in the academy is fingerprinted, photographed, and given a background interview. The investigative phase of the background process normally requires four to six weeks and includes a thorough check of police records, personal, military, and employment histories, as well as field reference checks. Candidates are evaluated under these standards: respect for the law; honesty; mature judgment; respect for others; employment record; military

A platoon of recruits stand at attention, holding their class banner, as they are paraded by a recruit platoon leader.

record; financial record; driving record; and use of drugs and intoxicants. All candidates must submit comprehensive biographical information prior to their background investigation interview.

Once the LAPD has determined that a candidate has met all of the initial requirements, is of sound physical health, and has a clean criminal history, the true fun begins. By this time, the application class has already dwindled by at least 50 percent, and the competition for the dwindling number of spots grows. An intense psychological examination is the next step en route to becoming one of LA's finest. Candidates are interviewed and evaluated by a city psychologist using psychological factors related to successful performance to determine if they are currently suited for the difficult and stress-

The badge, the decorations, and the honors—an instructor at the LAPD academy performs the tasks of teacher and role model for future Los Angeles Police Officers to come.

ful job of a Police Officer. "Why do you want to become a police officer?" might be a question that breaks the ice in an interview. The answers have varied from "I want to help people and keep them safe" to "I think it'll be easier to get women wearing a badge, a gun, and a neatly pressed uniform." One applicant, rumor has it, came to the interview in combat fatigues and packing his own .45, and said, "I tried for CHP (California Highway Patrol), but they said I was mentally unstable."

Getting into the academy for many is victory enough. It is a reward, though the grand prize, graduation and appointment to a command, is still elusive. Once accepted and inside the academy, the instructional phase looks more like military boot camp than law enforcement training. While the LAPD chooses to be somewhat tight-lipped about its curriculum for turning a civilian into one of the finest law enforcement officers in the country, the education consists of: extensive physical fitness training; study of the California penal system, legal codes, and the LAPD guidelines; firearms instruction and qualification (9mm and Remington 12-gauge shotgun); unarmed combat skills; basic computer and MDT operation; defensive and evasive driving skills; arrest procedure; handling of EDP (the politically correct term for Emotionally Disturbed Persons or what used to be known as psychos); and dozens of miscellaneous classes, courses, and instructional periods.

Graduation day is one of great celebration and fanfare. The unique LAPD badge, one of the world's most distinctive pieces of police insignia, is also one of the nation's most coveted. Wearing it, above the left breast pocket of one's uniform, is a badge of honor and proclamation that the police officer belongs to one of the most exclusive and respected organizations in international law enforcement. At each graduation ceremony, the Chief of Police addresses the new officers and informs them that their badge of honor is to be maintained at all times—and all that it stands for—is never to be tarnished.

Graduates of the academy are usually assigned to an area "somewhat" close to home (an officer living in the desert will probably not get assigned to work in the Valley), though officers that want to learn, want to become true cops in the old traditions, volunteer to serve in one of the city's rougher areas, places like 77th Street and Newton Area or Southeast Area and Rampart, where their skills, instincts, and courage can be tested. All those who graduate from the Los Angeles Police Academy are known as P-Is. P-IIs are the basic street cops, and P-IIIs, who wear two stripes, all having passed a series of supervisory tests, are semi-supervisors who evaluate P-Is for their job proficiency reports.

For a P-I riding in a patrol car, cruising the streets of the city with a seasoned partner serving as tutor and mentor, the mind has a tendency to wander and to recall the days and nights of hard work and studies at the academy. Only a few months ago that officer was covered in sweat as he pursued lap after lap on the academy track, honing his body and his mind. Today, he is watching jobs come in on the MDT, protecting and serving the citizens of Los Angeles. His daydreaming ends when a call coming through on the radio slaps him back to reality with a cold surge of adrenaline. "Any Hollenbeck units available, confirmed shooting on the corner of Wabash Avenue and So Street." It's a Code-3. A real job, and only the lights and sirens are more powerful than the rush of adrenaline pumping through the P-I's veins.

Over the course of the next year, and for the remainder of their lives, the officers will continue to learn and be tested—in the academy, as a Probie in their first command, and on the streets of the City of Angels.

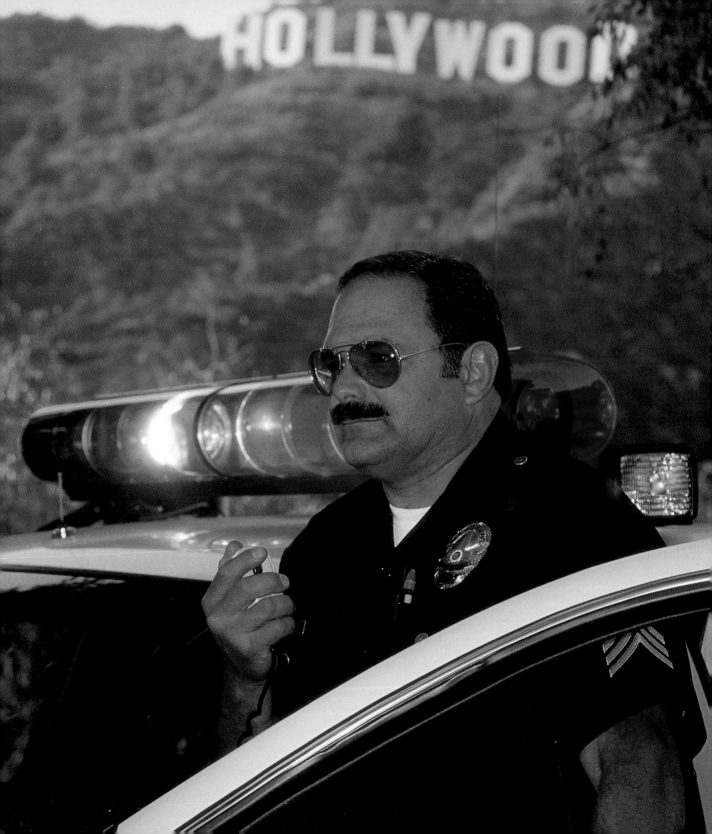

CHAPTER TWO

ON PATROL IN LOS ANGELES
The Essence of Police Work

The Los Angeles Police Department divides the city into 18 regional areas (known as precincts or districts in other police departments). They include: Central (1); Rampart Area (2); Southwest Area (3); Hollenbeck Area (4); Harbor Area (5); Hollywood Area (6); Wilshire Area (7); West Los Angeles Area (8); Van Nuys Area (9); West Valley Area (10); Northeast Area (11); 77th Street Area (12); Newton Area (13); Pacific Area (14); North Hollywood Area (15); Foothill Area (16); Devonshire Area (17); and Southeast Area (18). There are also several support areas, such as Metropolitan Division; the LAPD's elite force encompassing SWAT, Mounted, K-9, and VIP Protection; and Air Support Division, America's largest municipal police air force. Additional support areas are run out of the LAPD's nervecenter, police headquarters at Parker Center in downtown Los Angeles.

New York City might be known as the melting pot, but Los Angeles is a patchwork of diverse neighborhoods, cultures, socioeconomic standings, and geographic oddities all interwoven by freeways and highways spread out on both sides of the valley like a

giant mosaic. It is this diversity of cultures and languages, this wide gap of social standings, that many believe is the charm of Los Angeles. Where else can you go from Little Tokyo to Koreatown, the Barrio to Watts, and intermix Hollywood, "the Valley," and beach-freaks all within the confines of a single city. Police work in the city is just as diverse, and can be as different in Rampart Area, where whores, junkies, winos, and the poorer elements of life battle with gang-bangers, thieves, and the cops in a battle for turf and survival; to Devonshire Area, known as "Club Dev" because of its upper-middle-class homes and relatively low crime rate (though notorious for cop shootings). A cop walking a beat in Harbor Area is literally in another world from a cop answering calls in the notorious 77th Street Area. While the city is marked by diversity, the essence of the job, patrol, is linked by one ever-present constant—danger.

Patrol work has been characterized by police officers around the country—and, indeed, around the world—as hours of mundane routine interrupted by seconds of sheer terror. It is on patrol that officers respond to radio calls, despatches from central HQ, on anything and everything from crimes in progress to incessant car alarms. It is on patrol where the officers, riding in pairs, come into close contact with the citizens they protect and the citizens they need to lock

Sergeant Joe Klorman, Hollywood Area, answers a call with the famed landmark in the backdrop.

As backup is needed, a Pacific Area Officer requests his supervisor to the scene of an arrest.

up. It is on patrol where mutilated corpses are discovered, broken locks uncovered, and domestic disputes referred. There are no two days that are alike, no two jobs similar, and no shift immune from a possible Code-3. "The public views us in different ways depending in which context they see us," offers a female officer working Central Area. "If we cite them for a parking violation, we are a nuisance. If we respond to a mugging or a robbery, we are never there on time. If we respond to a domestic dispute, we are the enemy because we usually end up locking up one of the complainants who just might be the breadwinner. To many we are nothing more than donut-munching civil servants who care little for the people

we could protect. Nothing could be further from the truth, though it would be hard to convince anyone. I truly believe that the only way to change the public's image of what we do is to have them ride with us for a typical eight-hour shift. I guarantee that after they see what we do and go through on a daily basis, their perception of a police officer will forever be changed."

To an outside observer, working in Pacific Area's Beach Detail can be considered the "winning of the lottery" of police work. The officers patrol Venice Beach, where they are exposed to beautiful women, adoring tourists, and the trappings of sun, sand, and suntan lotion in the air. Venice is to many the true California. A place where beautiful people play in a

The black-and-white—the police car—is the most dominant tool of law enforcement in the LAPD.

serene setting and where a tanned body, a fast car, and the perfect set of sunglasses are all that is required out of life. Nestled against the Pacific Ocean, between Santa Monica and Marina Del Rey, Venice has become one of the city's trendiest places to visit. Initially designed as a copy of its Italian namesake, complete with canals, one-lane bridges, and gondolas, the picturesque reproduction was soon destroyed by development—namely the discovery of oil. In the 1950s, however, Venice became the hip spot for beatniks and escapees from mainstream culture, eventually developing into the Bohemian little piece of chicdom that it is now. Today, besides being the set for the mega-popular TV show "Baywatch," Venice is a place where visitors come to simply walk along the beach walk and observe the "California Crazies" and the eccentrics. There are skaters, and posers, showmen, and musclemen working out to the shuttering lenses of Japanese cameras on a daily basis. In the summer, when the weather hits the 90° mark, Venice Beach becomes a sea of human movement, as people strolling along the concrete walkway enjoy the cool Pacific breeze and the sights and sounds of one of southern California's most remarkable places.

Venice has a darker side. It is a known Mecca for transients, dopers, and certifiable mental cases who flock to the sandy shores in order to live on the beach. Many of these individuals are harmless and as colorful in their personality and charm as they are ragged and rough on the nose. Others, however, are dangerous. Many are intravenous drug users, and their needles are both means to score and means of self-defense. Many are disease ridden, some terminal with illnesses ranging from TB to AIDS. A good portion of them steal in order to survive. Some of them break into nearby homes to support their habits, others will hurl a lead pipe across a tourist's face in order to grab a purse or a wallet.

All the officers who work the beach are on a first name basis with many of the homeless who call Venice home. "That's Mary," claims Officer G. Grenadier, as he points to woman who is rambling to herself about President Reagan and hair spray, and who smells like a combination of the men's room at Dodgers Stadium and rotting vegetables. "She thinks she's married to Sergeant Frio," Officer Grenadier chuckles, as he says hi to "Jesus Christ," another local resident, and a man known as "Cisco" who is adorned with prison tattoos and was just released from LA County Jail after a stint for burglary.

The homeless and the crimes they commit are a routine facet of the day-to-day patrol work of the Pacific Area Beach Detail; fighting gangs has become one of the job's more dangerous aspects.

Venice is a magnet of humanity—a place where people come to hang out. It used to involve kids looking for members of the opposite sex, tourists looking for souvenirs, and families out for a bit of fun. Today, Venice attracts a completely different type of visitor— the gangsters. There is no turf to be fought over in Venice, no drug territory, but the beach has become a favorite hang-out for many of Los Angeles' inner-city gangs on the weekends—from Asian gangs in the Valley, to the Bloods and the Crips of South Central, to the Hispanic gangs of East LA It would appear that there would be nothing for a gang member to do in Venice other than enjoy the sunset and grab a burger, but life in Los Angeles just isn't that simple. Being a

The Pacific Area Beach Detail station—easy-going, carefree, and always busy.

gang-banger, as gang members are known, means always showing the flag and displaying the colors. It means a self-imposed sense of respect. Respect from your homeboys and utter terror from innocent civilians. When rival gang-bangers meet, be it on their turf or at a taco stand in Venice, the results can be deadly.

It usually begins with one gang-banger looking at a rival gang-banger's girlfriend. It could begin with something as stupid as a stare. But gang fights are no longer waged with fists and chains. They have become ballistic ballets of 9mm fire where everyone but the bad guy ends up getting hit. "These guys aren't marksmen by any stretch of the imagination, and their firepower has a tendency to hit innocent bystanders," claims a Beach Detail Officer as he checks his bullet-proof vest one final time before heading out on patrol. "The objective of our small unit is to respond to any large gang assembly immediately, to separate the knuckleheads from within pistol range, and then dissuade, detain, or arrest the troublemakers." Arrests of gang members on Venice Beach yields some incredible weaponry—from machetes with home made grooves to inflict even more horrific wounds than a "regular" eleven-inch blade could cause to Uzis, AK-47s, and even handfuls of antiaircraft artillery.

The man with his finger on the pulse of Venice is Sergeant Bill Frio who, in his light blue shirt, shorts, and sneakers, look more like a summer camp counselor than an LAPD supervisor. Sergeant Bill, as many of the homeless who live on the beach call him, is a no-nonsense kind of cop of the old school, but he realizes that his beat calls for different tactics and approaches to police work. The officers who patrol Venice are asked to instill a sense of hospitality and to both residents and visitors. Their special outfits help break the ice so to speak—and, as one officer commented, "it would be hard to fit in on the beach wearing our black uniforms." They appear less obtrusive and imposing in their beach fatigues, more like people looking out for one another than officers interested in making arrests. But Sergeant Frio never lets the officers in his command forget, even for a second, that they are police officers in a city beset by crime and violence and, occasionally, uncontrolled perversion.

Some of the wonderful individuals that the beach attracts enjoy walking up behind female visitors who are usually watching a street performer, and then forcibly rubbing against them until they've reached their surf-inspired moment of passion. These "Butt Boys" as the perpetrators are known is a growing nuisance, and one has latched himself onto a timid Japanese tourist who is too overcome by terror to scream or summon police. A passer-by with a cell phone dialed 911 and the Beach Detail races into action. Even though the officers surround the suspect, he is not about to let go of his mark and a small scuffle ensues with the poor woman caught in the middle. Seconds later, though, he is in cuffs and a resident of the Beach Detail holding cell where his paperwork is processed.

"This dichotomy of the many types of God's creatures who inhabit this stretch of paradise is what makes this such an interesting beat," claims a female officer completing her paperwork on an El Salvadoran charged with exposing himself. "You have people living in plastic bags only a few hundred yards from movie stars and Hollywood agents living in million dollar beachfront homes."

34

An armed-robbery suspect is cuffed by Officer G. Grenadier a block from Venice Beach.

Riding along the sand, the two officers stumble across two adolescent males, with guilty faces, who look like a wanted pair of thieves who steal handbags and wallets of the sunbathers. "Keeping out of trouble?" Officer Grenadier shouts from his window, as the two startled youth began to head back to the weightlifting area in the opposite area of the officers. Yet before Officer Grenadier and his partner can investigate the duo further, a Code-3 comes over the air. There is an armed robbery in progress at a nearby bank's ATM, and the regular black-and-white needs backup. The Beach Patrol's 4x4 kicks a cloud of sand as it fires up its engines, and sounds its siren and flashes its lights. As they make the transition from sand to pavement, the job comes over the screen of their MDT with further information—the assailant is reportedly armed with a 9mm automatic.

Seconds later, after twisting through the narrow streets across the plush canals, the officers reach the suspect who is being cornered by the regular patrol car for the sector. An additional set of hands and two extra 9mms are a reassuring comfort to the two officers, especially since the alleged perpetrator appears to be either a nut or high on methamphetamine, a popular narcotic on the West Coast. The man is refusing to place his arms behind his back, and is talking about "kicking a cop's ass!" As the officers draw their weapons and train their sights on the suspect, the two Beach Patrol cops move in and grab the suspect's arms in a forceful act of "muscle-inspired acquiescence." Onlookers stand in their tracks as they observe the ongoing arrest, but this isn't a show and the cops would much rather the civilians be out of the line of fire. "Where's the gun," an officer asks the suspect, his hands finally secured behind his back in cuffs, "What'd'ya do with the 9?" "I gots no gun," the suspect promises, "all I did was ask the lady for some change for a cup of coffee."

Encountering an armed suspect can happen in Pacific Area and it can happen in Southeast Area, one of the city's most dangerous. Anything can happen on patrol.

Each of the 18 LAPD territorial areas (once known as divisions) possess a special unit known as SPU (pronounced "Spew"), or Special Problems Unit, to handle a particular serious wave of crime affecting an area at one specific time. It could be push-in robberies, car-jacking, narcotics sales, or even prostitution, but SPU officers will be tasked solely with combating the one particular problem at any given time. They work their own selective shifts, they carry out their own warrants and sting operations, and are independent of the mundane aspects of police work that units out on patrol deal with. SPU squads handle only those radio calls linked to the problem they are working at any given time. The competition to get into a SPU squad is fierce. They are elites within the area, just like CRASH details (see chapter four), and only the best officers with the best arrest records are permitted in the squad. Of all the eighteen SPUs, the elite of the department is Sergeant Leo Kerchenske's Southeast Area SPU.

Officer Grenadier and his partner respond to a radio call while patrolling the surf and sand at Venice Beach on a windy spring morning.

Southeast Area is one of the more poverty-stricken areas of Los Angeles—a high-crime, gang-infested area where the murder, robbery, rape, and narcotics rates are way past what city politicians would consider acceptable. The LAFD (Los Angeles Fire Department) station across the street from the Southeast Area station house is one of the busiest in the city—and country—responding to more shootings, stabbings, and drug overdoses than any in the city. Southeast Area is also a melting pot. It is a United Nations of nationalities and gangs thrown together in a small enclave where one block is controlled by an El Salvadoran gang, the next one by a Mexican or Guatemalan gang, the next block under the ownership of a branch of the Bloods or Crips, and the block after that owned by Cambodian gangsters. The area's only notable landmark is Nickerson Gardens public housing project, considered by many to be the most dangerous stretch of urban landscape in the United States of America. LAPD officers are not permitted to walk its parameters alone, and every call to the "Gardens" requires at least two black-and-whites. "The gangs control the projects," Sergeant Kerchenske states as he removes his 9mm Beretta from his holster as he nears a Nickerson Gardens

courtyard. "They maintain a thriving narcotics industry here and they protect it with guns, Molotov cocktails, and even hand grenades."

The Nickerson Gardens used to be completely black and Hispanic, but in the early 1980s, the city, in its infinite wisdom, settled Cambodians refugees in the projects. The Cambodians, escaping the hell of war-torn Southeast Asia, soon found themselves in the hell of southern Los Angeles. "The black gangs," a SPU officer noted, "at first preyed on them like vultures on a carcass, but the Cambodians had been at war for the past 30 years and they knew a thing or two about fighting with automatic weapons. The Cambodians soon formed their own street gangs and with store-bought AK-47s and the knowledge of how to use them, they hit the blacks back with a deadly counterattack. Ever since then, nobody bothers the Cambodians."

As the SPU car pulls to a red light, at a corner owned by the "Pay Back Crips," an officer asks one of the gangsters, "Having any trouble with the Cambodians lately?" The OG (old gangster), in the required blue uniform of the Crips, shrugs off the question by saying, "S**t, them Cambodians are f**king crazy. Nobody messes with them."

"Are you strapped?" Sergeant Kerchenske asks the young hoodlum, a police colloquial for "are you carrying a gun?" "Are you hinked up?" Sergeant Kerchenske adds, using the street slang for "are you guilty of something?" On this cool night in March, Southeast SPU is after drugs and gang-bangers.

There are an estimated 5,000 gang members residing and operating in Southeast Area—all are into narcotics sales or thefts, all carry weapons, and all are, in the words of one seasoned LAPD Homicide detective, "trigger fingers without souls." They are not frightened of the police, undisciplined at home, and survive by a demented code of wanton violence and savagery the likes of which are incomprehensible to most. Gangs sometimes control several blocks at a time, sometimes one side of a street, sometimes nothing more than a few homes. They defend their turf

Officer Grenadier checks his MDT while receiving a call of a suspicious male exposing himself to a group of female tourists from Germany.

with AK-47s and Street-sweeper 12-gauge multi-round semi-automatic shotguns. They perpetrate drive-by killings, and firebomb the homes of potential witnesses. They discipline one another by drilling holes through the kneecaps of gang members who have stolen as much as a snort of cocaine.

Among the more violent of Southeast Area's gangs are: 80 Hoover Crip; 83 Hoover Crip; 90 Hoover Crip; 92 Hoover Crip; Ochentas; 87 Gangster Crip; Main Street Crip; 18th Street; Neighborhood Crip; Q102 Crips; Avalon Garden Crip; 107 Hoover Crips; 112 Broadway Crips; T-Zone Crips; Raymond Crips; E/C A-Line Crips; N-Hood Crips; Denver Lanes; South Los Carnales; 118th Street E.C.C.; Pay Back Crips; Gardena 13s; 165 Denver Bloods; Shotgun Crips; Swans; East Coast Crips; B-Bops; Circle-City Bloods; Front Street Gangsters; Athens Park Boys; Carver Park Crips; 89 Family Bloods; Kitchen Crips; Hoopride Crips; 89th Street East Coast Crips; Compton Avenue Crips; Colonial Watts Weigan; Hacienda Village Bloods; Bounty Hunters; Belhaven Bounty Hunters; Miller Gangsters; Imperial Courts P.J. Crips; and the Back Street Crips. The volume of gang activity is overwhelming to the area's CRASH unit, but SPU cops need to know much more than just the gang-bangers. They need to know where the serious narcotics trade is, the prostitution, the gambling, the auto thefts, and the burglaries. They need to be jack-of-all-trades in an area that grows bloodier on a daily basis.

"The basis for SPU," observes a Southeast officer, "is that no matter how many officers the LAPD despatches on patrol at any given time, the cops will always outnumber the bad guys. These are the odds that the system works under and will always work under. In order to even out the odds so that the goodguys have a chance now and then, the department has created this special unit that will battle the most serious crime wave taking place in an area at any given time." SPU cops don't answer routine radio calls. They respond to where their sergeant despatches them on high-visibility patrols against the heart of criminal activity in any given area.

It is a cool February evening in Southeast Area—far too cool for anything Los Angeles is used to. A sudden rainstorm and 40 degree temperature have done to the area what the criminal court system has so far been unable to do—keep the bad guys off the street. Sergeant Kerchenske enjoys the cool night and the smell of rain in the air. As a native of Cleveland, Ohio, the non-seasons of southern California cannot replace the endearing Ohio winters. But he knows that the rains will stop, and the gang-bangers and dope pushers will soon venture outside for trouble. Inside the station house, Sergeant Kerchenske discusses a warrant going down for the following day with two detectives toting 12-gauge 870 Remington shotguns. The detectives, burly men trying to balance their case of evidence and criminal reports with the weight of the shotgun, ask Sergeant Kerchenske for a few minutes of his time so that some manpower details can be worked out. It isn't going to be a large raid, those are reserved for Metropolitan Division and SWAT, but tactically, nothing is ever left to chance in the LAPD. "One of the Crips is known to always carry a pipe-bomb, you know," the detective remarks to his partner as they contemplate on how many officers to bring to "the party." "S**t," his partner replies, "I think we should notify someone from the bomb-squad just in case."

Another gang specialist confers with Sergeant Kerchenske as well. He is the area's CRASH sergeant and is known by every gang-banger in Southeast Area as "Crocodile Dundee." Not for his exploits battling crocodiles in Australia, but because he is British, a for-mer London bobby, and his Cockney accent sounds closer to the movie character's Australian drawl than anything they've ever heard before. "Crocodile Dundee" is a brilliant cop, a Gang Professor, as many call him, but some of the officers tend to laugh as they watch him and a gang-banger, one used to talk-ing in the cryptic dialogue of the inner city, attempt to carry on a conversation. Some of the Cambodian gangsters he deals with think he works for the CIA. Many of the Hispanic gang-bangers are convinced he is really an immigration agent.

"Crocodile Dundee" hands Sergeant Kerchenske several Polaroid snapshots of two black males, Crips, who are "dearly" wanted in the area for a drive-by killing. "A CI [confidential informant] has told me that J.J. might be hanging around at "Fig and 104." The CI also said that he carries a Mac-10 in a gym bag, but others have told me its a Tech-9."

Although the evening shift is well past roll call and its initial tour of its sectors, the officers in Southeast SPU have yet to hit the streets. Two officers are searching for a wanted felon in the NCIC com-puter, while another is searching through files for a witness's name in a drug case that involves the Nickerson Gardens. By 6:00 P.M., after the paperwork is complete, the officers grab their gear and head to their fleet of patrol cars parked out back. After he checks his shotgun and grabs a fresh battery for his radio, Sergeant Kerchenske follows his troops out on the streets to handle the area's special problems. As they leave the station house, the LAFD fire house next door swings into activity as an ambulance races south toward Artesia Boulevard. Sergeant Kerchenske checks his screen thinking that the call might be gang

Gang graffiti, the mark of territory in Southeast Area.

related, but it isn't. A husband and wife, tired of looking at each other on the cold night, decided to drink, have sex, and then fight. The wife ended up with a broken jaw. The husband ended up with a steak knife in his calf muscle. Patrol units take down the reports.

Patrol for a SPU squad means cruising locations marked by very distinctive boundaries that most outsiders to the area wouldn't be able to distinguish all too clearly. "Gang graffiti is like cats pissing on furniture to mark their territory," a SPU officers comments as he notices a Crip tag marked with a black "X"—the sign that a Crip has been targeted for a drive-by. There isn't a building, a mailbox, a pay phone, or even a fence that isn't marked by the spray-paint signature of the criminal underground.

Sergeant Kerchenske's patrol pattern differs from day to day, all dependent on who he is after and what crimes patterns are being attended to. But he always tries to pass an alleyway in the southeastern-most portion of the area, one that borders the county and the domain of the Los Angeles County Sheriff's Office, where a young mother of three was carjacked and then gang-raped by El Salvadoran gang-bangers. The case was one that is known in the area as a gut-wrencher. The gang-bangers not only raped the woman in front of her young daughter, but did it right behind their house, where their gang graffiti was prominently displayed. To this day, he cannot forgive the perpetrators for their heartless cruelty, and he cannot understand their stupidity for doing their crime so close to home. "These thugs are only feared because they are vicious," Sergeant Kerchenske points out, "certainly not because they are geniuses."

As he ponders over the case of the raped woman, a call comes over area radio summoning SPU to a home near Wilmington. SPU officers on patrol stumbled across a wanted suspect, a Blood, known for his brisk marijuana sales. The officers found the suspect in front of his house drinking a pint of malt liquor and then ordered the 18-year-old male to raise his hands and assume the position. He threw his bottle on the floor and raced through the house, into the yard, into the darkness of a frigid Los Angeles night. A search of the house, conducted with the consent of the suspect's father, yielded a gun, some rock cocaine, bags of marijuana, and enough $5 bills to choke a horse. Narcotics investigators were called in, but the gang-banger escaped. It wasn't a good night.

Throughout the evening shift, in fact, Southeast SPU handled nearly a half-dozen drug sellers—some were apprehended and brought back to the station for booking. Others, at the first sight of "5-0," the gang term for the police, ran off into the darkness.

At 2:00 A.M., as the shift is ending and another day comes to a close, Sergeant Kerchenske and his officers are summoned to the Nickerson Gardens for a shooting. A Hispanic male, in his thirties and known to the police as a drug seller, was shot in the back and buttocks as he walked outside. His wounds appear to be serious but not life-threatening. By the time Sergeant Kerchenske reaches the scene, an LAFD trauma team is already stabilizing the patient and Southeast detectives are canvassing the area for shells and witnesses. "Hey Sarge," one of the detectives smiles, as he greets Sergeant Kerchenske, "slow night, eh?"

While 2:00 A.M. may be the slow part of the graveyard shift in many areas (bars in Los Angeles serve their last rounds at 1:45 A.M.), it is the busiest times in the Los Angeles Area in which to patrol the legendary Hollywood Area. Like the city, Hollywood Area encompasses a true melting pot of cultures, races, languages, religions, and social statures.

In the Hollywood Hills, along Mulholland Drive and Laurel Canyon, you have million-dollar homes owned by Hollywood's elite—from Madonna to Sharon Stone. Less than a ten-minute drive from the opulent driveways and stucco exteriors, on Sunset Boulevard, crack-whores (women who are addicted to the rock) perform oral sex on johns for a $10 bill. It is an area in which the Manson family killed Sharon Tate and where John Belushi died of a drug overdose. In Hollywood there are the Dragons, the "he-shes," the transvestite prostitutes who work on Sunset and

Sergeant Leo Kerchenske points to El Salvadoran gang graffiti that marks a back alley where a young mother was car-jacked and brutally raped.

Hollywood, and, of course, there is the legendary Walk of Fame along Hollywood Boulevard and the human waves of tourists who make the pilgrimage to Grauman's Chinese Theater to see if their feet are larger than John Wayne's. Hollywood is one of the few areas of Los Angeles that doesn't die at night. The opposite happens, in fact. During the days, when there are robberies and assaults almost everywhere else in LA, Hollywood is relatively quiet. Hollywood is a creature of the night. "It is surreal here," claims one patrol officer, "it's as if the people here are vampires by the hours they live by."

City planners have been working relentlessly to rebuild Hollywood as a safe place for tourists to visit. Removing the "geeks, freaks, and hookers," according to one officer, is a primary objective of the department. The geeks and freaks, it was studied, are attracted by the hookers . . . so the policy was zero tolerance for prostitution. If the hookers go, the politicians, community leaders, and business groups argued, their traffic will go as well. And with the criminal element gone, it was hoped, the boulevards of Hollywood will be treacherous no more.

The evening shift begins with roll call, and the day shift is happy the day is over. It is Friday, usually one of the busiest days of the week, and the front desk has been a turnstile of humanity and chaos with complainants, the confused, and the convicted. "Hollywood Area, my name is Officer Jones, how may I help you?" the desk officer says as he attempts to decipher the ramblings of a call directed to the front desk. "Your son has beat you and sold your dog, Ma'am?" The officer asks as he begins to jot down a few notes, "Oh. . . . your son beat the dog and sold your jewelry? Can you please talk slower? Hello? You want a ride to the Safeway? Hello? Are you still there?"

As the phone traffic intensifies, so too does the amount of people coming in off the street. A 93-year-old man, walking slow but with a definite sense of unbridled dignity, walks into the station. Tugging at his tie, he asks the black officer working the phones if he speaks Armenian. "No sir, I am sorry, I'm originally from Alabama," the officer remarks, hoping to illicit a smile in return, but all he gets is, "Excuse me, do you speak Armenian?" While an interpreter is sought, a woman walks in, both eyes black and blue and tremendous bruises on her upper arm. "Excuse me? Where is the detective in charge of sex crimes?" she asks, her question drowned out by the screams of a Russian cab driver, wondering why his taxi was ticketed while parked in front of a no parking sign. "I AM A TAXPAYER DAMNIT, I AM A BUSINESSMAN, AND I WANT A WRITTEN APOLOGY FROM YOUR CHIEF!" the outraged hack shouts, as he pounds on the desk with a forceful smack of indignation. "Sir," Officer Jones replies with incredible restraint, "our chief does not handle tickets, and secondly, could you please refrain from pounding on my desk." At the same time, a call comes through from a woman who sees a man with a sawed-off shotgun entering her neighbor's house. "I'll send a unit over there immediately," the officer promises, "just stay on the line please."

Just another day in Hollywood Area. Soon, night will come and the true spirit—and madness—of the area will intensify.

Guns found in a suspected drug dealer's home.

Tonight's roll call is a bit larger than most and involves officers who are wearing different uniforms than the strict LAPD attire, carrying different firearms, and wearing different badges. In order to clean up the prostitution, patrol in the area will be augmented by several dozen Chippies, the nickname of troopers from the California Highway Patrol. Friday night is cruising night down the neon-lit boulevards, and prostitution, sex crimes, robberies, and other usual LA craziness are to be stopped this evening. The state of California could send in the National Guard to try and stop the hookers in Hollywood, but they wouldn't have half as much success as the area's PED, or Prostitution Enforcement Detail, a twenty-man unit designed to aggressively patrol the streets of Hollywood and put the hookers and their Johns out of business.

PED, a section within "Hollywood Vice," has done a remarkable job in the few years since it was formed. Successes range from hooker sweeps to arresting such prominent celebrities—and noncelebrities—as actor Hugh Grant and semi-celebrity Joey Buttafuoco for their encounters with ladies of the evening (or in Joey's case, a vice detective dressed up as one of LA's working women). They have gath-

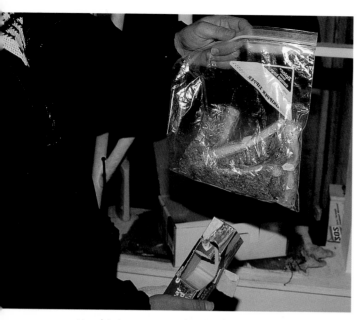
No, this is not oregano! A Southeast Area narcotics detective holds up a bag of marijuana, seized at the home of a gang suspect sought by SPU officers.

ered over the years extensive files on just about every known whore in the area—from men working as women, to women working for crack, to men working as men. All sexes, all sexual persuasions, and all the different varieties are handled identically. They are identified, cataloged, and when enough evidence exists, arrested.

PED, because it takes in the best officers of the area into a single unit, is also a backup SPU unit of sorts despatched to sensitive problems where police firepower and special police diplomatic skills might come into play.

Following the area roll call and a much-needed dose of high-octane coffee, Sergeant Steve Vinson, a 15-year-veteran and PED supervisor, provides an impromptu roll call for his officers. The shift will last from 6:00 P.M. to after 4:00 A.M. and the objective is to go after hookers not already on file. There was a time when the officers would have to be blind in order *not* to see a hooker. There were once hundreds, some estimates say as many as thousands, of girls/men working the boulevards of the area. The number of whores has dwindled since the inception of PED, but the patrolling efforts remain intensive.

Hollywood (movie and TV Hollywood, that is) has created a glamorous impression of the world of prostitution that is lucrative, alluring, and filled with happy endings. Nothing could be further from the truth. The girls or men are filthy, disease-ridden, and miserable creatures selling their dignity for a pimp's pleasure or the demon of crack cocaine. Policing the hookers is dangerous business and the PED officers take nothing for granted. Hookers, many of them intravenous drug users with a wide array of communicable diseases, are volatile and precarious—and many work the streets when they are high on meth, crack, or PCP. Many of the johns might be wide-eyed tourists or middle-class professionals, but other johns are sadistic felons out for a pipe-cleaning before perpetrating another crime. Some, arrests have shown, have even been serial killers. The hookers also have pimps who patrol the streets collecting cash and making sure that their stable is productive and keeping in line. While pimps tend to be businessmen, they will resist arrest—often violently—if they feel they are about to lose some cold hard cash. "This is real dangerous work," offers a PED officer as he checks his 12-gauge shotgun. "Some of these girls will kill you in a blink of an eye. And I'll be damned if I am going to let my guard down for even a split second as I approach a whore and her john on a traffic stop. I have a wife and two kids at home. I intend to come home in the early A.M. without a knife wound, a bite mark, or a gunshot blast."

With the famed Hollywood sign overshadowing the streets below, the PED officers head to their cars for the night's work ahead of them. Some cruise the streets in black-and-white patrol cars; others, hoping to catch a whore or a john with their guards down, patrol in unmarked, beat-up sedans. On Sunset Boulevard, not far from where Hugh Grant was arrested, a Dragon, a colloquial term for a "Drag Whore," is seen walking slowly up the boulevard gazing at the oncoming traffic. Sergeant Vinson and his partner, Officer Bill Pack, swing their cruiser around in a 90° turn and cut off the Dragon who is acting as if he/she was just walking on the street minding her/his own business. "What's your name?" Officer Pack barks at the whore, as he fastens a pair of work gloves to his hands. "Carrying any needles? Ever been arrested by us? Where are you from?" The Dragon begins to cry and to tremble. Obviously, the fear of lock-up and the fear of being away from the rock are beginning to take their toll.

When the pressure on streetwalkers becomes too much of a hindrance to business, new and more innovative approaches of plying the world's oldest profession spring up. One of the more recent tricks is for the hookers themselves to cruise the boulevards in rental cars paid for with stolen credit cards. As they pull into an intersection for a red light, they solicit the johns awaiting in the next lane.

Hookers are a symptom, a cancerous tumor to the overall health of the crime situation, but they are not the sole ailment plaguing Hollywood. Sometimes even the wealthiest people are a cause of criminal concern. As the PED officers process a female prostitute

A female officer, responding to a past assault between neighbors (an argument over drug money), returns to her patrol car to file a report.

and run her through the system before she is taken to county jail, a call comes through from the Hollywood Hills concerning a wild party going way out of hand—loud music, cars blocking driveways, and the smell of marijuana lingering throughout the air. But because the party is being held in a $2 million mansion and because the complainants all live in similar homes, this becomes no ordinary call. Rich people are very precarious when it comes to law enforcement. They can become abusive, even violent, if told "not" to do something and are habitual letter writers, complainers, and litigants, claiming police brutality if, according to one officer, "the cop doesn't get on his knees and do some serious ass-kissing." But million dollar homes are also rented to record companies and even drug gangs for wild parties. So the potential for violence and danger always exists.

Climbing up the steep and twisting hills, up Laurel Canyon, Sergeant Vinson and his PED task force encounter a grid-lock of illegally parked vehicles. There aren't any Hyundais or Subarus parked on the winding streets, only BMWs, Jaguars, Mercedes-Benzes, and Corvettes. As they near the source of the trouble, Sergeant Vinson's windshield begins to vibrate and pound as if being confronted by a supernatural force. In essence it is—twelve mountain-size loudspeakers conveying a deafening dance beat to an army of men and women who have far too much money and far too much spare time on their hands. The PED task force responding to Laurel Canyon doesn't know what to expect and realizes that a party full of liquor and semi-obnoxious people can result in bedlam. As they assemble at a staging area, Sergeant Vinson advises his officers to remove their Kevlar Fritz helmets and visors from their trunks and to ready their batons—when past parties have had to be broken up, responding officers have had bottles and rocks hurled at them. At the entrance to the location, a complainant wearing a bathrobe and visibly upset by the unstoppable decibel assault he faces meets the officers. "I'm going to f**kin' kill someone if these misfits aren't thrown

"Yes Ma'am, it is safe to walk here!" A concerned visitor to Grauman's Chinese Theater, recalling the old Hollywood, finds a reassurance in the presence of so many officers on a street once known for danger and decadence.

thrower discusses the predicament with Sergeant Vinson, some of the city's beautiful people begin to assemble hurling insults at the officers. "Rodney King, Rodney King," shouts a nerdy guest of the party as he dangles his Rolex watch in front of the officers. "Look Ma," yells another, "it's the goon squad." Sergeant Vinson and his officers display remarkable—unbelievable, in fact—restraint and professionalism in handling the situation. In any other city, in any other police force, some of the beautiful people would have been instantly rendered not so beautiful as their dental work was rearranged by a nightstick. "Sir, this is your house and you have the right to throw a party, but you do not have the right to interfere with your neighbors," Sergeant Vinson says in a truly diplomatic voice of authority mixed in with respect, "so the music has to be turned off and what's more, the Fire Department will be up here in a few minutes towing vehicles that are illegally parked and blocking emergency roads." The threat of a tow can bring even the glitziest people to acquiescence. Slowly, the partygoers leave the shindig headed for their cars and the mad search for legal parking. As the ensemble walks past the cops, some are barely able to contain their laughter; it is a parade of the elite, the surgically altered, the brash, and the opulent. A 400-pound Arab sheik walks hand-in-hand with two semi-naked women, a midget is seen on the shoulders of a 50-year-old woman looking like a cross between the Bride of Frankenstein and Ernest Borgnine. Each guest departing throws a double-side air kiss at the host. It is all so phony. It is all so Hollywood.

Within an hour, the party has ended, the cars have departed, and not a single civilian complaint filed. It's been a good job, but there are still another three hours of patrol left, and the post-midnight hours are when the hookers do their best business.

Back at the station, Sergeant Vinson returns for a quick bit of paperwork and a talk with the watch commander. As he enters the station house through its rear entrance, he notices one of the Vice unit's sergeants, an undercover, talking to a girl sitting out-

out of here," he yells, venting at the officers simply to vent at someone. "I understand sir," Sergeant Vinson says as he tries to walk the complainant back to his house, "we'll take care of everything."

Sergeant Vinson asks for the party organizer and the house owner, and he is greeted by a 30-year-old white male clutching a champagne glass and a pompous attitude. As the homeowner and party-

Another Dragon is "handled" by PED Officer Bill Pack. "Get off the streets now," the officers warn, "or you'll be locked up!"

Responding to a stabbing on Melrose, a Hollywood Area patrol car races Code-3 from its post on Hollywood Boulevard.

Metropolitan Division Officers, on a crime suppression patrol, talk to detainees (suspected gang-bangers and rock sellers) in South Central Los Angeles.

side the holding cell cuffed to the bench. The plain-clothes sergeant is in no mood for a game of 20 questions with the girl, whose breath smells of semen. "Were you ever arrested in California?" She begins to cry a bit, and then curse, wanting a cigarette and a warm meal. "Damnit I hate whores," the sergeant replies, "they'll never answer straight to anything."

Back on the streets, Sergeant Vinson and his squad continue to patrol and make arrests. A Dragon is picked up outside a 7-11 on Sunset Boulevard for attempting to turn a trick behind the slurpy machine; two males are arrested in a brand-new BMW for marijuana possession; and an old man, claiming to be a

grandfather of seven, is arrested after he is caught masturbating in the intersection of Hollywood and Vine.

It all may be routine, but there is never routine in police work—especially in Los Angeles. Inside the immaculately clean hallways of the Hollywood Area police station, on the wall near the armory, is a black-and-white poster, sitting in plain view for all to see. It states, "It started in Hollywood, and ended in the Onion Field." It is a reference to the notorious March 1963 killing of a Hollywood police officer and the eventual subject for a best-selling book by Joseph Wambaugh. The poster is a reminder to the officers serving in the area—from the newest probie to the watch commander—that even though they serve in a diverse area with flashing neon lights, hookers, and rich people, the dangers of police work are there at every turn.

On the night of October 22, 1994, Officer Chuck Heim, temporarily assigned to Hollywood from his detail with the Mounted Unit over at Metro Division, and his partner, Officer Felix F. Peña, followed up on a tip in search of a known gang-banger wanted for dealing drugs out of a motel room in one of the darker corners of Sunset Boulevard. The two officers approached the suspect's room in the run-down Dunes Motel with caution, and knocked on the door forcibly. "This is the Police, Open Up!" The suspect's girlfriend quickly opened the door but as Heim entered first, he was shot at point-blank range in the head. Officer Peña was hit in the hand, his gun hand, before he could fire back. While the suspect continued firing, another responding officer braved the fusillade of bullets and pulled his two wounded comrades to safety. Fearing that the suspect was still held up in one of the rooms, possibly holding hostages, SWAT was called to the scene as was K-9, and provided aerial support from Air Support Division choppers.

Officer Heim was rushed to Cedars-Sinai Medical Center where he died a few hours later. Heim's wife, also a police officer, served with him in Metro Division as well.

Officer Heim's funeral was attended by thousands of police officers from all over southern California, as well as from as far away as Vancouver, British Columbia; Dallas, Texas; and New York City. At police funerals in Los Angeles, it is customary for an officer to lead a riderless horse in the funeral procession. This time, however, there wasn't going to be a horse in the ceremony—leading the horse was always Officer Heim's job. Only a few months earlier, in February, Officer Heim led the riderless horse at the funeral of rookie Officer Christy Hamilton, cut down in cold blood by a teenager with an assault rifle in Northridge.

"Danger is part of the work, part of the job, and part of the reason why we are out here," claims a ten-year veteran as he fastens his shotgun in its vehicular mount at the start of his shift. It is midnight on a warm autumn night, and the life of the patrol officer continues. Rampart Area is a treacherous 18-square-mile stretch of low-income real estate that is home to a large percentage of the city's alien—resident and illegal—population: Koreans, Guatemalans, El Salvadorans, Cubans, Mexicans, and tourists, workers, and visitors from just about every corner of the globe. There are an estimated 500,000 people crammed together in the dense abyss of Rampart, and it is one of the highest crime areas in the country—one block in particular,

Having completed roll call and received his list of assignments, an officer checks his shotgun and takes it to the assigned black-and-white that'll be his mobile office for the next eight hours.

at Sixth and Alvarado, is considered the most treacherous street in the country. Rampart Area is as close to the old LAPD as one can find—a frontier post policed by officers who are no-nonsense, professional, and always aware.

On a ten-to-six, the midnight shift, Rampart officers can respond to a dozen shootings, half a dozen ODs, and enough violence and misery in an eight-hour time period to last a lifetime. "Sure I can make almost twice as much money being a cop in Santa

47

Barely out of roll call and yet to check his 12-gauge weapon, a Newton patrol officer receives word of an armed robbery in progress.

It is 4:00 A.M. on Los Angeles' skid row, just off of Sixth Street in the area covered by Central Area. There is a small homeless city where transients and drunks live off of hand-outs and church-supplied balony sandwiches. Two Central Area patrol cars are summoned by a burglar alarm at a beer warehouse off of Sixth Street. In the parking lot, near some empty boxes, they find the cause of the alarm—the suspect is young, clean shaven, and banging a lead pipe against his head while screaming at a high-pitched wail. The officers, their Beretta 9mms out and aimed at the suspect, approach with caution and fear. If he's high on PCP, he could sustain ten gunshot wounds and be high enough to literally rip the officer's throat out. If he's mentally challenged, or deaf, and does not understand the police orders, any potential shooting might result in an Internal Affairs hearing and possible proceedings. As two other officers approach, one cradling a Remington 870 in her arms, another officer produces a can of mace from his utility belt and when he gets within range, unleashes an intense stream of the spray into the individual's eyes. It has no effect. He's high on PCP and begins to hit his skull even harder. Blood is now spraying in all directions, and the officers fear for their safety.

As the officers inch closer to the suspect, their fingers depress their triggers ever tighter—wanting to

A patrol car's rear windshield shot out by a 9mm, creates a night full of paperwork for the officers who were the target of the drive-by.

Ana or Huntington Beach," claims the ten-year veteran, but these streets are the Harvard University of law enforcement. A rookie can learn more police work on one shift in Rampart than he can with 20 years on the job somewhere else." Another Ivy League school of California law enforcement is 77th Street Area, in the south, that encompasses much of South Central Los Angeles. It was in 77th Street Area, on a routine shift on patrol, that the riots erupted at Florence and Normandie.

A Central Area patrol car cruises along 4th and Flower, in the heart of the business district downtown.

be ready if that split second of judgment is needed and the suspect needs to be taken down. The department will review shootings to determine whether the officers have violated any firm policies, and reviews are to be avoided at all costs. LAPD officers can use deadly force:

- To protect themselves and others from immediate death or threat of death or serious bodily injury.
- To prevent a crime in which the suspect's actions jeopardize the safety of others and risk them to death or serious bodily harm.
- To apprehend a fleeing felon for a crime involving serious injury—or death—and only if the suspect runs the risk of injuring or killing others if he/she is not stopped immediately.

In the parking lot, all the criteria exist for the police officers to use deadly force, but nobody wants to shoot the individual. Nobody wants to kill the suspect, but nobody wants to be eulogized, either.

In the parking lot, a tense game of creeping forward continues, as chaos quickly erupts. A chopper flies low overhead, shining its powerful searchlight atop the suspect, and a pit bull, a pet of another resident of the street, has entered the parking lot and begins to menace the officers. "Get that dog out of here or I'll blow its f**king head off," a sergeant screams at the dog owner as he trains his Beretta on the growling dog's head, "get it out now, or I'll kill the f**king beast!" The homeless man begins to cry and scream, fearing that his one friend in the world is about to get a one-way ticket punched to doggy heaven. The side show is just the diversion that was needed, however. The PCP-head stares for a second at the barking dog, and an officer pounds his wrist with a baton causing the lead pipe to fall to the ground. Before the PCP-head can recover from the strike, he is underneath five officers and his hands are cuffed behind his back.

"I love patrol," comments an officer at the beer warehouse happy that no triggers were pulled. "One minute I'm in a five-star hotel taking a complaint from a lingerie model worried that her jealous boyfriend stole a suitcase of her bras and panties, and the next minute I am arresting a psycho covered in s**t and blood. Anything can really happen!"

49

CHAPTER THREE

LAPD SWAT
The Nation's First and Finest

The office is the definition of chaos in motion. Inside a room barely large enough to hold five, ten men, their sizes increased by gun belts sporting Colt .45 automatics and biceps that have been pumped up to granite proportions, sit around manning the phones and jotting down notes. The walls are sparsely decorated—a chart, a calendar, and plaques—wooden and pewter words of gratitude from some of the best and most secretive fighting forces in the world—from the U.S. Navy's SEAL Team SIX and the U.S. Army's 1st SFOD-Delta to the French GIGN and the Israeli *Ya'ma'm*. Six sergeants sit at a bank of phones that for some reason on this Wednesday afternoon keep ringing without letup. A constant stream of officers enter and then exit, some clutching the latest weapon from Heckler and Koch, others holding enlarged photographs of a crack-den. It is well-choreographed, non-stop movement, and something's brewing. The unit, although scheduled for training the following day, is on standby awaiting a warrant to simultaneously hit several drug locations in South Central Los Angeles

LEFT AND RIGHT: During rescue training in breaching a barricaded location, SWAT officers deploy an explosive charge to burst through a front door of a training field's "killing house." *Courtesy: Sergeant A.R. Preciado*

"It's a go for tomorrow," claims Sergeant Al R. Preciado, the unit's senior sergeant known in the unit vernacular as 20-David, "we are on for the warrant." "Outstanding," is the reply, "simply outstanding!"

Every organization has its elite, and within every elite is a small cadre of professionals who set the stan-

SWAT officers fire a Starflash munition through the bathroom window of a targeted narcotics location in Southeast Area's notorious Nickerson Gardens.

dards and raise the level of skill and motivation for everyone else. For the LAPD, the elite is its Metropolitan Division, a six-platoon force based in the epicenter of one of the most squalored portions of Los Angeles, inside the headquarters of Central Area near the city's skid row. Metropolitan Division is the LAPD's special operations division, its special-forces command of sorts, that fields highly specialized units tasked with everything from hostage rescue to VIP and dignitary-protection details. Yet the true legends of Metro Division are its tactical operators. The officers of D Platoon. Welcome to the world of the finest police (and military for that matter) tactical unit around—the Los Angeles Police Department's SWAT Platoon.

To most Americans, the term SWAT denotes the image of heavily armed police officers, clad in body armor and pumping shotguns, kicking in the door of a crack house, or arresting a dangerous

The SWAT patch.

A cast-iron door is yanked off of its frame during a warrant served at a drug location in South Central Los Angeles. *Courtesy: Sergeant A.R. Preciado*

felon wanted for a string of violent crimes. Hollywood has only reinforced this image of a military-style police unit responding to the most desperate and violent criminal confrontations. After all, SWAT stands for Special Weapons and Tactics, but in reality nothing could be further from the truth. In police circles, among the men who actually suit up when the uniform officers require backup, and who load the 12-gauge double buckshot rounds into shotgun chambers, SWAT stands for something very different it mean Sit, Wait, And Talk. The tactics they employ are to save lives, their own and the perpetrators they are charged with neutralizing and apprehending. SWAT officers would rather bore a criminal to death than shoot him, and firepower is used *only* as a last resort. On the streets of Los Angeles, California's glimmering City of Angels, the last resort means that the city's SWAT unit will be on the scene—whether that means safeguarding the 1994 Soccer World Cup tournament in the Rose Bowl to serving a warrant on a drug gang dispensing poison to the ghetto.

Long before the 1972 Munich Olympic Massacre, long before hostage-taking became a terrorist art form, the LAPD realized that certain outbreaks of public violence and certain criminal situations required more than an officer with his .38 in one hand and a bull horn in the other; in many of these high

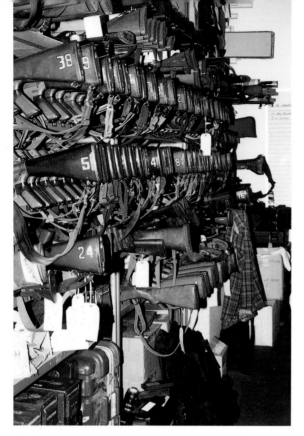

The SWAT armory.

police officer's old trusted 12-gauge shotgun just would-n't do. The 1965 Watts Riots were a true turning point in the city's history. For a department that had reinvent-ed itself into a modern, innovative, and para-military-like force of highly professional officers capable of meet-ing any challenge, the changing and extremely violent face of the American inner city had taken the LAPD completely by surprise. Cops weren't peacekeepers caught in the middle of civil unrest during the 1965 riots, they were targets. Many of the long-time residents still refer to the outbreak of uncontrolled violence as "the uprising," an assault against authority, and the LAPD found itself under the gun like never before. "Fighting crime is a far different ball game than fighting for control of a city," reflected one retired detective work-ing Watts at the time. "The situation was a war zone." The most pressing problem that most officers faced dur-ing the riots was that of ending up in the crosshairs of a

rifle. Snipers targeted cops and killed several officers in cold blood. The department required a small, highly mobile force of officers who would function as a group of virtual soldiers embedded in a civilian police agency. The man who pioneered this revolutionary theory in modern policing was a young commander named Daryl F. Gates. Gates was a transitional figure—a protégé of Chief Parker—he was old-school LAPD. Yet he was an innovative thinker who realized that the "thin blue line" of officers was all that stood between a modern func-tioning metropolis and chaos. Thus SWAT was born.

Gates realized that the LAPD would need a unit that could raid fortified locations, need to be expert in urban tactical situations, and be as proficient in a wide assortment of large-caliber automatic weapons and firearms as a conventional combat soldier. Urban unrest in the 1960s wasn't restricted to Los Angeles, Gates real-ized, and for the next riots, calling in the National Guard took time and eventually cost civilians—and cops—their lives. Initially, Gates' main concern was to have at the ready a mobile force of officers who could deal *tactically* with snipers. The unit was to be an informal one of vol-unteers, officers who patrolled their usual beats during normal shifts but could be summoned at a moment's notice to respond to any developing situation. Officers who volunteered for this new and mysterious unit got no extra pay, no special bonuses. All they were required to do was carry their "lunch," the code word for rifle, in the trunk of their police cars.

The LAPD SWAT unit was first trained in the art of tactical warfare by elements of the United States Marine Corps. Fearing another large-scale riot, the unit needed to acquaint itself with the "recapturing of the city." The Marines, already owners of extensive combat experience from Vietnam, were ideal instructors—there was always an internal LAPD joke that should the city be taken over by the criminal element, SWAT would be in the vanguard of the counterattack by assaulting the city through its sewers. Yet the image that Hollywood has produced of the icon LA cop, spit-and-polish and polite in his black uniform and mirrored glasses, was far from the reality of the initial SWAT training. Armed with rifles, SWAT vol-

During tubular assault training to teach officers the fine art of rescuing hostages from a hijacked bus, SWAT officers deploy a flash-bang before making their dynamic entry. *Courtesy: Sergeant A.R. Preciado*

Lieutenant Runyen (left), 10-David, confers with one of his officers prior to serving and arrest warrant.

unteers spent endless hours marching through the storm drains of the city practicing ways to move through the city undetected. That period was a time what many veterans call "Old SWAT," and although the unit never had to retake the city from the storm drains, the turbulent and violent path that America was taking would, in hindsight, prove just how right Gates was in creating a special weapons and tactics element within the department.

On December 9, 1969, SWAT officers attempted to serve felony warrants at the party headquarters of the Black Panther Movement—a black power group that had engaged in extremely aggressive and violent criminal activity peaked by the murders of police officers in several large cities. When the unit arrived at the fortified location at 41st Street and Central Avenue, they were greeted by shotgun blasts and the explosive successive bursts of automatic fire. For the next five hours, Black Panthers and LAPD units exchanged over 5,000 rounds of ammunition in a melee that resembled a battlefield rather than a city street. It was chaos sparked by the glow of ordnance flying through

the night and spent shell casings littering the streets. It was also one of the wacky situations where a major blood bath could have happened, yet there were no fatalities to either side. Eventually, the combination of the SWAT unit's dedicated firepower and the fact that the Panthers had virtually run out of ammunition led to their surrender. Remarkably, nobody was killed in the battle, although three officers were hurt and one Panther received slight wounds.

In LAPD circles, the Black Panther incident was the end to what would be known as "Old SWAT." The

With the skyline of downtown Los Angeles in the background, a senior SWAT officer looks on as he reviews an assault technique, while clutching his Benelli 12-gauge shotgun.

A briefing at Metro Division HQ is offered just prior to a large-scale warrant. The SWAT unit, Southeast CRASH, narcotics, and a large representation from the division all listen in for the tactical details of the morning's "mission."

part-timers and the rifles in the car was a stopgap, but the city needed more. The department required a unit that could work together and train together on a full-time basis. In 1971, Chief Davis authorized the creation of the SWAT Platoon. It wouldn't be a club of volunteers and war vets with their own heavy firepower, but an integral element of the department's Metropolitan Division. Training would no longer be covert, at night, and in the city's sewers, but a full-time endeavor meant to turn an officer endeared with the A-to-Zs of conventional policing into one who could fast-rope down the side of a building, storm through a barricaded location full of hostages, and become the city's force of last resort in incidents that the "regular" cops were ill-prepared and not trained to handle.

The unit would not have to wait long until it was tested in "battle." On May 17, 1974, the unit participated in the most notorious fire-fight in the city's history when 19 SWAT officers descended on a house on East 54th Street in the heart of South Central Los Angeles where they believed that kidnapped heiress Patricia Hearst was being held by the radical Symbionese Liberation Army (SLA). Two SWAT squads armed with shotguns and automatic rifles closed in on the residence and surrounded it, but the

SLA terrorists inside did not respond to the bullhorn and the order to surrender and to leave the premises peacefully. A SWAT officer anxiously clutching the bullhorn with one hand and his rifle in the other gave the residents of the house a remarkable "twenty-five" chances to surrender. Each plea was met by deafening silence. As tensions mounted and the possibility of a confrontation grew inevitable, a tear-gas canister was fired into the house. The SLA responded with machine-gun fire. It was a hellatious fire-fight, the likes of which had never been seen before in an American city. For the next two hours, 54th Street was a war zone. Carried to a local audience live on TV, the shoot-out looked more like a chapter from the Wild West than a scene from the capital of the new American West. The deafening blasts of gunfire and ricocheting rounds engulfed South Central. Hundreds of officers had to be called in for crowd-control duty to keep the curious and the foolish away from the battle. The 19 SWAT officers received additional supplies of ammunition courtesy of LAPD helicopters flying support missions.

Eventually, the house caught fire, and the six SLA gunmen inside opted to die in a blaze of gunfire and black smoke rather than surrender. Inside the charred remnants of the house, police and FBI agents found an arsenal of rifles and submachine guns, over 6,000 rounds of "unspent" ammunition, and two pipe-bombs. "The fire-fight at the SLA headquarters," reflected Sergeant Al Preciado, who at the time of this book's writing is the unit's senior sergeant and unit heart-and-soul with over thirty years on the job, "was definitely the scariest thing I'd ever been involved in."

The incidents at 41st and 54th Streets were of tremendous significance to the SWAT unit—a transition from the past into the future. In fact, the numbers "41" and "54" are engraved elements on the LAPD SWAT patch. Both incidents, in their own specific ways, were ballistic wake-up calls as to how things should be done and proved that large-scale tactical incidents should not "go down" with a barrage of gunfire like a shoot-out in a B-movie Western, but rather a deliberate,

Sergeant Al Preciado examines the rope and hitch to the SWAT Suburban just before the unit learns that the warrant is hot and heavy and a go.

57

A fully equipped SWAT officer is formidable opponent for any suspect.

precise, and professional assault or response where the officer's training, equipment, and abilities permit him to safely handle the situation with finesse. Fearing that there would be groups more dedicated and dangerous than the SLA to hit the streets of Los Angeles in the future, SWAT commanders realized that the platoon would have to become a cohesive squad of specialists, akin to a U.S. Army Special Forces A Team or even a U.S. Navy SEAL Team. In fact, LAPD SWAT would train regularly with the U.S. Army Special Forces community, as well as the SEALs. As the cutting edge of police tactical units, LAPD SWAT believed that less was more, speed more important than brute force, and professionalism and training a religious and life-saving code that would personify every aspect of their job. As a result, admission standards to the unit were significantly raised and tightened, discipline enforced, and greater respect shown toward the community. It was not easy meshing these military and civilian law enforcement requirements into a viable entity, but LAPD was successful, and the SWAT unit became a national role model.

Remarkably, the unit is small by big city standards—only 67 officers with the commanding officer being a lieutenant. A sergeant commands each squad which consists of two five-man elements, with each "element" commanded by a Senior Lead Officer. All element members are "operators," expertly trained assault specialists with several members cross-trained as snipers and observers. Interestingly enough, the first LAPD SWAT snipers weren't expert gun enthusiasts, but rather officers who owned their own high-powered weapons. When not on a tactical job, SWAT officers operate in uniform or plain clothes in unmarked police cars on anti-crime assignments. One of their busiest roles has been in issuing high-risk felony warrants to the city's most dangerous wanted men and women—a task that has become more hectic and voluminous in the past few years.

In the first decade of its existence, the SWAT Platoon had proven itself by tactically solving hundreds of volatile situations in the city—from armed felons holding hostages in a bank, to serving high-risk warrants on drug locations. Through their training, their work, and their professionalism, they developed a sense of confidence and mission that would become part of their mystique and, as many in the unit would comment, "their charm as well." Yet the man who had the most confidence in the unit's abilities was Los Angeles Police Chief Daryl Gates, who not only recognized their ability and impregnable character, but also knew that there wasn't a challenge that the officers of the platoon couldn't handle. When Los Angeles was selected as the sight for the 1984 Summer Olympic Games, Police Chief Daryl Gates announced that the SWAT unit could handle any and all outbreaks of terrorism within the city limits even though the Federal Bureau of Investigation had just created its own counter-terrorist and hostage-rescue unit to deal with any such incidents. It was a bold statement, and many thought an overly confident one. Without a doubt, SWAT was a truly specialized police unit, but it had yet to train in the delicate art of counter-terrorism. In fact, Lieutenant Jeff Rogers, a remarkable officer who commanded the unit for 13 years, even told his commander that, "We are a SWAT team, not a counter-terrorist outfit!"

If D Platoon was to truly be in charge of counter-terrorist intervention at the 1984 Summer Olympiad, then the unit would need to embark on a hurried refresher course in the art of stopping terrorists determined to turn a global sporting event into a political message emblazoned with the blood of innocents. It was just ten years since the 1972 Munich Olympic Massacre, and the images of masked gunmen holding the world hostage was carved in the minds of the game's planners and city officials. More importantly, though, were the images of the dead hostages, their charred bodies still strapped into a German Air Force helicopter, that would become icons forged in the psyche of the SWAT commanders tasked with supervising the massive security blanket covering the games.

Chief Gates quickly despatched his three most trusted SWAT and Metro Division officers—Lieutenant

A SWAT and Metro officer practice the removal of the ladder from the Suburban transport vehicle.

Rogers, Captain John Higgins, and Sergeant Al Preciado—to embark on a globe-trotting counter-terrorist crash course studying the tactics and equipment deployed by Israel's *Ya'ma'm* (national police counter-terrorist unit) and *Sayeret Mat'kal* (the Israel Defense Forces' "military" counter-terrorist special forces unit), Italy's GIS and NOCS, France's GIGN, a U.S. Army Special Forces counter-insurgency team operating in West Berlin, GSG-9 and other German state *Speziale Einstaz Kommandos* or SEKs, and the British SAS. The three Los Angeles officers returned from their trip full of ideas and a long wish list of equipment, gear, and weapons that they would need should they truly be able to meet any terrorist attack launched during the Olympic games. The

gear required included special tactical poles with mirrors on the ends for use in around-the-corner situations inside or around buildings, and the pioneering use of flashlights attached to shotguns, assault rifles, and automatic pistols. To prepare for the challenges of keeping the peace during the Olympics, the unit also entered into a joint training course with the U.S. Army's 1st SFOD-D at Fort Bragg; similar arrangements were established with the U.S. Navy's SEAL Teams, including the enigmatic SEAL Team SIX. Much of this security instruction was also dedicated to VIP and dignitary security—both in plain clothes and in full tactical gear.

Prior to the 1984 Olympics, the SWAT unit generally trained with blank rounds in its then-limited tactical assault course. Once counter-terrorism and hostage-rescue entered its job description, the unit began to train in abandoned buildings using real bullets. Here they could learn the art of hostage-rescue by hitting mannequins substituting for terrorists while not hitting hostages and not getting hit in the crossfire of *live ammunition*. In preparation for the 1984 games, the unit fired more rounds of ammunition and threw more diversionary devices (also known as "Flash Bang") in several months of instruction than they would have in 20 years of "regular" training. The games in Los Angeles went off without incident, partly due to the vast American law-enforcement and intelligence effort to locate and identify potential terrorist threats, and partly due to the deterring reputation of the unit. Even though various military special forces and the FBI's Hostage Rescue Team were on call in Los Angeles during the games, , the 1984 Olympics was the first time in modern Olympic history that the overall tactical security and counter-terrorist responses were the responsibility of a municipal SWAT unit.

Because of its multifaceted responsibilities and its early "blow-em-out, shoot-em-out" confrontations with the Black Panthers and the SLA, LAPD SWAT has always taken great pride and unique consideration in selecting and modifying the firepower they carry. The side arm carried by all LAPD SWAT officers is the Colt government model .45 automatic—a heavy piece of firepower that is far more daunting than the average 9mm automatic carried by the rest of the department. SWAT opted on the heavy-caliber weapon because it was found that on tactical deployments, when lethal firepower is needed, that bullet mass, diameter, and momentum are more important than the bullet's design, velocity, and kinetic energy. It was also found that on combat shooting courses, officers could shoot better with the Colt .45 than they did with any other weapon tested. Yet even though the caliber of the weapon was suited for SWAT's needs, the weapon still did not meet SWAT standards, and like everything else that the unit possesses, the Colt .45s were modified by the platoon's armorer (a man considered by many to be

A stoic portrait of a SWAT officer, completely adorned in his load-bearing equipment and body armor, with an MP5 slung over his shoulder.

Armed with a high-powered Hurst tool to literally rip doors off their hinges, a two-man entry team readies itself for their role in the five-pronged warrant.

and each officer attends a *minimum* of four training days a month qualifying with the .45 during which he will fire an average of 200 rounds. Beside the three basic drill courses that the officers must score highly on, they are also trained in advanced tactical drills, such as shooting on the move, engaging moving targets, one-hand shooting, pistol retention drills, transition drills (from shoulder weapon to .45), malfunction drills, multiple target drills, speed reloading, flashlight technique, prone positions, kneeling positions, barricade positions, target discretion problems, and hostage-rescue targets. According to one New York City officer who visited the SWAT platoon, "These guys do more shooting in a month than most departments do in a year!"

The .45 is the primary SWAT weapon used for routine patrol and crime suppression, building searches, and during operations in confined spaces. For dynamic assaults and entries during warrants, the unit's primary tool is the Heckler and Koch MP5 9mm submachine gun. The MP5 is the mainstay entry weapon of just about every SWAT unit in the United States, and just about every police tactical team in the world. It is the Rolls Royce of submachine guns, and one of the most accurate, durable, and reliable weapons ever designed. Much lighter than most of the other submachine guns around, the fact that it fires with a closed bolt affords greater accuracy—even when fired in the full-auto mode. The only thing that many senior SWAT officers didn't like about the weapon was its caliber. One internal SWAT report even indicates that the unit would have "preferred" the system to be available in a .45 caliber. To increase its stopping power, SWAT policy is that the weapon be fired at full auto, in two-shot bursts, at ranges of ten yards or less.

The support weapon used by SWAT is the Colt CAR-15 5.56mm assault rifle. A highly reliable weapon favored by special forces from the U.S. to Israel, South America to Great Britain, the CAR-15 is a compact and extremely accurate weapon that can lay down a blanket of covering fire from considerable ranges. The CAR-15s are primarily carried by the unit's commanding officer and its senior sergeants.

the genius behind its operational abilities). Modifications included fixed high visibility sights, a 4-pound trigger job, lowered ejection port, beveled magazine well, polished feed ramp, throated chamber, and an ambidextrous safety latch for left-handed officers. SWAT was also the first police force to introduce a small flashlight to the frame of a weapon that is activated by a pressure switch mounted on the grips.

SWAT doesn't expect its officers to be average shots with the .45s—it demands that they have pinpoint accuracy. Weapons proficiency is a religion in SWAT,

Two shotguns are carried by SWAT. The first is the Remington 870—a pump action 12-gauge workhorse that is, perhaps, one of the most popular shotguns in service today. The "870" was the first shotgun issued to SWAT officers in its early years, but the pump-action, especially during the elongated chaos of a hellatious fire-fight, was found to be cumbersome (it is, however, still carried in every LAPD patrol car). Under the ballistic proving grounds of the mean streets of Los Angeles, the 870's pump-action was somewhat difficult to fire from a prone position, and nearly impossible to fire with one hand. The 870s are still used, but today they are mainly deployed for the firing of diversionary munitions, such as the highly-effective Starflash, or for blowing doors off their hinges. The primary SWAT shotgun is now the Italian-made Benelli 12-gauge M1 Super 90 (with a plastic stock and a forward pistol grip), as well as the Benelli 121-M-1 recoil operation semi-automatic. "The Benelli is a masterpiece of ballistic handiwork," claims a SWAT P-III as he readies his gear prior to a warrant. "It is easy to fire, accurate, and ideally suited to our needs." The Benelli sights are zeroed for a center hold at 50 meters with one-ounce slugs, and patterned at various distances with "00" buck magnum ammunition. Virtually all of the Benellis are fitted with a mini-flashlight attachment.

In D Platoon there are 12 observers and snipers. They are summoned for VIP protective details and for call-outs when a barricaded perpetrator is held up in a location, or someone is holding hostages. Observers are part sniper, part tactical officer, and as a result, are responsible for providing suppressive fire at reasonable ranges during live-fire engagements. Sniper positions, or "high-ground" as they are known in the vernacular, are usually established farther than 100 meters from a targeted location. The platoon's 12 observers are issued with two shoulder weapons. Observers used to be armed with the Heckler and Koch HK 33 5.56mm assault rifle, but the M-16A2 and CAR-15 5.56mm assault rifles have now become the weapon of choice. Observers also carry a bolt action Remington Model 700 .308 sniper rifle with a 3x9 scope. On a "typical" (no two are really ever the same) call-out involving a barricaded subject, the observer will be responsible for gathering intelligence for the sniper and unit commander, as well as providing a protective perimeter for the snipers.

LAPD SWAT snipers are legendary in the American police community, and, as a result of the platoon's contact with units around the world, their reputation has carried into the international police and military community as well. The primary sniper weapons are the American-produced .308 and .223 "Special Marksman Scoped Bolt-Action Weapon" by Robar. The unit's former sniper weapon, the Heckler and Koch GSG1 7.62mm police sniper rifle, is now used primarily for night operations, and fire fire-suppression missions.

In terms of personal equipment, SWAT officers are prepared for any and all contingencies. Each officer is issued with a two-piece Nomex flame-retardent combat suit, specially adaptable load-bearing gear, and Point-Blank Tac vests with insertable ceramic plates to meet any high-velocity ballistic threat. Standard SWAT headgear, in addition to the black balaclava, is a black Fritz helmet equipped with an integrated Motorola personal radio earphone/microphone combination.

Like everything in Los Angeles, the lifeblood of the unit is the vehicle. For their "routine" (if you can call hitting the streets of Los Angeles "routine") crime-suppression details, the unit patrols in a small fleet of unmarked and black-and-white vehicles. Because a call-out can happen at any moment, often at the most inopportune time, SWAT officers carry all their personal gear in the trunks of their patrol vehicles. Call-outs, when the unit is deployed anywhere within the confines of the City of Los Angeles, will usually bring about the SWAT truck, a bread-truck-type vehicle that acts as a mobile arsenal and communications post. When the unit deploys on a warrant, the usual mode of transportation is a small fleet of "dark blue SWAT Trucks" (actually GMC Step-Vans and Suburbans) that can quickly and comfortably transport the operators to all points in the city.

The vehicles are in tip-top running order. They have to be, for on a good day, just to get to a call-out in one of the more northwest areas of the city can take as long as forty minutes without traffic. The Suburbans have specially-modified rear bumper rails that afford for a chaindevice to be attached so that front gates and fortified bars can literally be ripped off. For use during warrants and other specialized duties, Secret-Service-like extension floor panels have been added so that the officers can ride on the exterior of the vehicle to a targeted location, or provide some added "available" firepower during a VIP protection detail. Special hooks have also been added to the vehicles to allow them to carry the ladders the platoon often employs in reaching a second story of a targeted location. Another specialized LAPD SWAT vehicle is the "Simms Mobile," named after Larry Simms, an officer in the unit. The Simms Mobile is a pickup truck with an added rear-seating area and a hydraulic ladder emerging from the rear cargo hold. Capable of reaching as high as three stories, the objective of the Simms Mobile is to drive a squad of officers toward a location, prop the vehicle against one of the walls, and then have the officers climb up the ladder and execute a dynamic entry though a window.

In the mid-1980s the unit began using a pair of battering ram-equipped small armored cars, known as the V-100s, but their deployment stirred some controversy about a military vehicle being used in a civilian law enforcement situation. Although a court order is required for its deployment in a warrant-serving situation, the unit deploys it immediately and without question when shots are fired at either officers or civilians and mobile armored protection is required.

If LAPD SWAT is anything, it is a unit that professes a religious adherence to professionalism, physical fitness, and firearms proficiency. LAPD SWAT does not accept just anybody. Unlike other police departments, a hook (better known in some police vernaculars as a "Rabbi") will not get you into SWAT. Your father could be the mayor or Chief of Police and it wouldn't help. Service in D Platoon is based solely

Ladders up and ready, SWAT officers make their dynamic entry into a second-floor apartment.

on merit, skill, desire, and ability. Even a volunteer to the unit must be in superb physical condition before the officer can even be considered for a spot on the force. All the volunteers must be from Metropolitan Division, must have a proficiency rating in the top 25 percentile within the entire force, and must have four years of experience on the force with a minimum two years of "field experience." Only officers whose courage on the streets is beyond question and whose service jacket is impeccable (from discipline to attendance) are even considered for a spot in SWAT. SWAT team members are expected to be able to run the most elaborate and exhaustive of close-order-drill military obstacle courses and must achieve a passing grade on the course on a quarterly basis. The training course, which includes everything from small arms to the history of guerrilla warfare, lasts seven weeks.

Californians worship the outdoors and physical fitness like no other segment of the American population, and that Golden State ethic is a golden rule in SWAT. The adherence to a strong physical fitness doctrine began, in earnest, in 1984 while the platoon was preparing for the Olympics. It has since become the unit's routine regimen. SWAT officers spend 240 hours a year honing their weapons skills, and perfecting their climbing and rappelling capabilities. The thought process behind this strong body philosophy is simple: because of the extremely arduous tasks that SWAT is faced with, from climbing up a building to rappelling down from a chopper, an officer who is not in top shape is a danger to himself and the rest of the squad. The policy doesn't dictate that an officer be a muscle-bound strongman capable of bench-pressing 500 pounds (even though a good percentage of the officers have biceps as large as a hill and necks as wide as a boulevard); it simply means that they should be able to run a rudimentary physical fitness test. In fact, a large percentage of the officers in D Platoon are lanky, thin, and carrying just enough muscle to keep their pants up, though possessing the strength and agility of a gymnast. SWAT policy also dictates that each officer, from 10-David, the title for the unit com-

mander, to its newest member, undergo a physical fitness test four times a year. The examination consists of a combination of pull-ups, bent knee sit-ups, push-ups, and a three-mile run.

To the unit hierarchy, the physical examination is a bureaucratic necessity. The unit spares no expense and no effort in training its officers. On one winter's morning, the platoon's climbing cadre embarked on an obstacle course training session at an abandoned aerospace factory in Northridge, in the confines of Devonshire Area. Led by Sergeant Preciado, the cadre established a heart-pounding, muscle-aching obstacle course for all the officers to pass and then run the course (which included everything from a building climb to a 100-meter run) in less than fifteen minutes. One of the officers, in running the course in an incredible eleven minutes, looked disappointed by his performance and his "mediocre" time. "Geez," he told a buddy, "I shouldn't have had the eggs for breakfast or I could've shaved thirty seconds off my time."

To train the platoon's officers, SWAT will send its officers to Camp Pendleton to train with the United States Marine Corps. They will also head to U.S. Army and U.S. Navy installations in the Mojave Desert for live-fire training. The platoon conducts heliborne insertion and fast-rope exercises with the U.S. Navy and the LAPD's Air Support Division, and they are as adept in sliding down the landing skids of a chopper as is any "counter-terrorist" operator in the world today. Like counter-terrorist squads in Europe, LAPD SWAT is trained to fire from moving choppers. It is a poorly-kept secret that the platoon has trained with both Delta Force and SEAL Team SIX at fairly regular intervals—and many in both Fort Bragg and Little Creek NAB will grudgingly admit that the military units tend to learn more from the LA cops than vice versa.

Since their inception in 1966, the SWAT unit has been deployed over 1,000 times in some of the meanest streets in America, where gang-bangers usually pack heavier firepower than the average officers. SWAT deployments fall into four distinctive categories: (1) call-outs or responding to jobs where sus-

Under the menacing glare of two officers armed with a .45 and a CAR-15, two drug suspects acquiesce to being handcuffed and secured.

pects are barricaded or holding hostages; (2) serving high-risk warrants; (3) VIP protection details; and (4) crime-suppression details and support of other Metropolitan Division units. Operations are known as "missions." Assaults are known as "rescues."

"Call-outs" are the true definition of what a SWAT team is all about—the ability to summon, at a moment's notice, a force of highly-trained professional tactical officers that can respond to and resolve any dangerous criminal situation where hostages or barricaded suspects are held up. The purpose of having SWAT respond is *not* to end a job with weapons ablaze and a high body count. Lethal force is a means of absolute last resort. "We are here to save lives," claims the SWAT commander Lieutenant Runyen as he returns from serving a warrant in Southeast Area. "This is deadly business and my guys have to know that there will come a time when they'll need to pull the trigger, and they'll need to do so based on their instinct and the fact that they feel that the bad guy was threatening them or someone else, not only when I'm right behind them telling them its OK." On numerous jobs SWAT has employed non-lethal devices such as bean-bag, Stinger, and foam-rubber rounds.

Unlike other SWAT units around the country, SWAT does not have the resources and manpower to allow a hostage or barricaded situation to take forever to wind itself down. The city is simply too big, the department too busy, and the unit too small. Most "rescues" are resolved in four hours or less, though certain incidents have been known to go as long as ten or twelve hours.

The unit lives by its radio (always turned to the TAC-1 frequency), cell phones, and beepers. In the last few years, some of the unit's most impressive call-outs have included:

- On the morning of May 4, 1988, a resident of Compton named Reynard Jones walked into a Westside high-rise office building, and without any provocation grabbed a hostage and took her to one of the top floors; the suspect claimed to have a bomb on him, and would blow up the building if he didn't get a car and $5,000 in cash.

His finger on the trigger, and a 12-gauge "00" magnum round in the chamber, a SWAT officer secures a perimeter while the interior of a location is secured.

SWAT was immediately summoned and they prepared a tactical resolution to the problem while an officer attempted, unsuccessfully, to convince a bank teller in the lobby below that he needed $5,000 in order to end a hostage crisis. The bank teller, of course, refused the request so the officer, as dedicated to the mission as they come, inserted his bank card into the ATM, and withdrew a significant amount of the money himself.

For the next several hours, Sergeant Mike Albanese, an experienced veteran of the unit,

Following a successful entry where the target was breached with no difficulty and none of the officers hurt, Sergeant Preciado (center) debriefs his men.

negotiated with Jones—first getting him the "cash-advanced" money, and then haggling over the car. Jones was terrified about getting a .45 slug through his head (he was reported to have offered each of the responding officers $100 *not* to shoot him), though he refused to surrender as well. As Sergeant Albanese had Jones on the phone and ordered the wily bomber to look out

the window and see the car, SWAT officers detonated a flash-bang grenade outside and burst through the door. Jones was arrested, the hostage released unharmed, and the $5,000 recovered.

• On the morning of October 20, 1992, Tan Khuat, a down-and-out father who had been smoking rock cocaine and downing beers for the better part of a night decided that he wanted to kill himself and his family. Officers surrounded the area and SWAT was summoned from the downtown headquarters upon learning that Khuat was armed and holding his three-year-old daughter hostage. He was determined to kill himself and his daughter "heart-to-heart" by shooting her and himself with the same bullet. A SWAT sniper raced to an elevated firing position while hostage negotiators and SWAT officers tried to buy time until the marksman had a clear shot. Khuat was inititally holding a revolver to his daughter's head, and a plan to bring him outside where he'd be vulnerable appeared to be paying off. A SWAT officer delivered some food to the front door and Khuat, still clutching his child and his gun, came out to retrieve it. As the sniper peered down through his scope and readied his trigger finger, Khuat bent down to pick up the bag of burgers and fries. The sniper fired a single .308 round, aimed directly at the center of the suspect's brain, that missed and pierced his left ear. Shot, angry, and intending to end it all, Khuat retreated into his apartment to complete his murder/suicide. The officers stormed the house and found Khuat in a bathtub, holding his daughter close to his heart and screaming, "I'm going to kill the baby!" He never got the chance. Officer Joe Cordova fired one round from his MP-5 at Khuat's head, right beneath the eye, killing the man instantly.

• At 5:30 P.M. on June 12, 1994, two young men armed with automatic pistols robbed a liquor store in the city's downtown area, pistol-whipped the clerk, and then fired several shots into the store's ceiling before getting away with some cash. Before they could make their getaway, however, a black-and-white sector car of the city's Metropolitan Division received a call of a robbery in progress and, with its sirens ablaze, headed to the alleged scene of the crime. The robbers, now in flight, opted to make a break for it. They stormed into the Western Medical Clinic brandishing their weapons and promising the frightened staff and patients that they'd kill everyone if they told the police where they were hiding. The black-and-whites called for the SWAT unit and a stand-off ensued. The SWAT officers, wearing their black Nomex coveralls, black Kevlar body armor, and Fritz protective helmets, quickly established an outer-perimeter (where the uniformed officers kept the crowds and press at bay) and an inner-perimeter (from where the search for the perpetrators would begin). An observation team and a sniper set up an Observation Post atop a nearby building and entry teams were coordinated to methodically and systematically search for the two gunmen. The utmost care was to be taken, as it wasn't known if the robbers were just hiding or holding their weapons to the heads of hostages. None of the officers wanted to engage in a firefight, but full loads were squeezed into the chambers of several 12-gauge shotguns and full magazines loaded into MP5s. Floor by floor, room by room, the SWAT unit searched the facility. With a helicopter on scene buzzing the complex and the SWAT team closing in, the gunmen did the only thing that was prudent. Surrender. At 10:15 P.M., nearly five hours after the ordeal began, the two dazed and bewildered suspects were cuffed and led away to the station house before heading out to the county jail. Unheralded and with little fanfare, the SWAT team gathered its gear and personnel and returned to quarters. Another "job" successfully in the log book.

Also contained with the SWAT team are members of the LAPD's Crisis Negotiation Team (CNT) who provide both verbal and tactical support to SWAT team elements during barricade and hostage incidents. For large-scale operations, a Tactical Operations Center (TOC) is called on to direct operations and deployments. On all jobs where SWAT is despatched, the SWAT commander and Metropolitan Division captain assume command and control of the entire situation. It is a harsh responsibility with sometimes far-reaching reper-

His firing hand never far away from opening the flap of his .45's holster, a SWAT officer looks on as the investigating detectives begin their work.

cussions. It should be pointed out that the now-infamous O.J. Simpson car chase was a SWAT call-out job. Initially, there was talk of landing a force of officers on the freeway in front of the moving Ford Bronco and ending the ordeal there, but in the end SWAT officers were stationed inside the Brentwood estate; a SWAT sniper, in a ghillie suit, in fact, had camouflaged himself inside O.J.'s immaculate garden and was ready to drop the suspect should he have raised his gun at any of the responding officers. Luckily for O.J. Simpson, he dropped the gun

before a sudden movement would have been considered "threatening by an armed perpetrator" and handled accordingly.

In 1996, SWAT responded to an impressive 57 SWAT call-outs. Some can happen two to a night, others happen virtually once a week. In 1996, the number of rescues is slated to an astounding 70 call-outs.

There isn't a job that the unit enjoys more than what is referred to simply as "a warrant." The purpose of a warrant is to gain entry into a location and seize the evidence. A warrant means that a good percentage of the unit will suit up, ready for battle, and travel to a location targeted by a particular area for a dynamic entry. Most warrants that eventually wind up on the desk of Lieutenant Runyen deal with narcotics—the gang-bangers who deal in crack, methamphetamine, and heroin are all serious players in the drug business. The gang-bangers carry firepower that many times makes the weapons carried by SWAT appear "small caliber." They have a propensity for violence, and they also have a knack for fortifying their drug stashes with heavy cast-iron bars and fences, booby-trapped floors and ceilings, and inches of bulletproof glass.

There is no municipal police tactical unit in the United States or even the world that prepares for a warrant like the LAPD's SWAT Platoon. Their approach goes beyond the professional ethics taught at the academy and the tradition that has become a living rule book on the streets. It is military in nature. Watching the platoon prepare for a warrant is like watching a Marine Corps battalion readying for an amphibious landing. Equipment is checked, intelligence is reviewed and double-checked, and each man is tasked with knowing his job to the letter, through instinct, and without hesitation. In other police departments, briefings can take anywhere from ten minutes to a few seconds. Dynamic entries to these departments are routine and common. Only with LAPD SWAT are aerial photographs used for intel, and architectural blueprints studied with meticulous zeal.

It is chilly in Los Angeles, it's early March, and the typical balmy 75 degree weather has yet to make an appearance. But at Metro HQ, where weather patterns rarely dictate the workload, the cool temperatures are soon to be replaced by a hot and heavy warrant. 77th Street Area narcotics has come across a leading member of the inner-city's rap music industry and SWAT is needed for the entry. The mission is not a sure thing, however. 77th Street narcotics has a small force of detectives in an OP (Observation Post) observing the targeted location, and a CI (confidential informant) has promised that the wanted individuals will be on the premises with both a cache of guns and a drugstore full of narcotics. The detectives on the case, nervously fidgeting about the Metro Division briefing room toting Remington 870 shotguns, aren't looking for a bullshit arrest. They want to catch the suspect and his girlfriend carrying enough narcotics and weaponry so that even a plea-bargain will land them in San Quentin for a very long time.

The briefing lasts for nearly an hour as every facet of the warrant is covered. Sergeant Al Preciado, 20-David, sits atop a table, his utility belt worn snugly on his waist, looking over the aerial shots. Sergeant Lamprey, another one of the senior SWAT sergeants, briefs the unit on the protective plexiglass used inside the location for the ad hoc recording studio the two have set up. The plexiglass is bulletproof and is a cause of great concern.

Following the briefing, the officers head to the parking lot where they fetch their Benellis, MP5s, and CAR-15s, as well as breaching tools, ladders, halogen tools, battering rams, and ropes. They will drive to the parking lot in the Southeast Area station house where they will assemble, suit up, and await word from the detectives in the OP. For various reasons, the warrant must be executed by 7:00 P.M.—otherwise it's going to be an abort! As the clock ticks past 5:00 P.M. and then on to 6:00 P.M., tension mounts. Lieutenant Runyen and Sergeant Lamprey both commence a dual cell-phone assault on the narcotics commanders, as the narcotics detective in charge of the warrant begins checking with the OP on a secured frequency. The officers are tense, but use a dry and often caustic wit to ease their nerves. The officers might have done but all this a thousand time before, each warrant brings about new dangers, new fears, new potentials. "You'd have to be nuts not to be scared," claims one officer, "but being prepared is a sure-fire antidote to letting your emotions overtake what needs to be done professionally."

In many circles SWAT stands for Sit, Wait, And Talk. In this case, as the warrant is scrubbed, the acronym stood for Sit, Wait, And Thank you very much—you won't be needed tonight. 7:00 P.M. has passed and Lieutenant Runyen instructs the platoon that tonight's fun and games is an abort. There will be a next time.

Although power bars were scoffed down, cans of Coke devoured, and a pool of adrenaline that could fill a lake pumped in the veins of the men, the officers weren't disappointed. They've been called off a thousand times before, and will be called down a thousand more times in the future. "It's part and parcel with the job description," claims an officer as he removes his Kevlar vest and tosses a halogen entry tool and a battering ram back into the trunk of his black-and-white, "but you'll see," he adds, "tomorrow we'll be going down hot and heavy and today will be all forgotten."

In the course of a year, LAPD SWAT carries out over 50 warrants—virtually one a week, and no two are ever the same. The warrants are not for "little ol' ladies from Pasadena" with outstanding jay-walking tickets. They are for some of the city's—and country's—most desperate and violent felons. Gang-bangers whose body count sometimes reaches into the dozens, narco-terrorists dealing in $1 million of narcotics on a weekly basis, and murderers who sleep with Uzis under their beds. When SWAT gets a warrant, it is known as "departmental last resort."

The objective of SWAT in handling a warrant is to get the job done without getting any of the officers hurt or killed. The targeted location has to be reached quickly and stealthily, the dynamic entry must be made quick and forcefully, and any potential threat must be dealt with tactically. Beyond having to worry about getting shot or shooting someone, the SWAT officers have another consideration—when targeting a drug location, they must get to the evidence before the bad guys. The unit could storm a crack house with the dexterity and dynamic movement of a well-choreographed commando squad, but if a kilo of cocaine gets flushed down the toilet and the gang-bangers walk because of lack of evidence, it's all been for nothing. The officers might get pumped before each tactical assignment, their biceps might flex, and their adrenaline might begin to thrust through their veins, but unless the operation yields arrests, evidence, and firearms, there is bound to be disappointment back at Metro upon the unit's return to HQ.

Captain Bud Lewallen's last day as the commanding officer of Metro Division was supposed to find him in his office for no more than an hour or two to collect a few momentos, and turn in his uniform and process his paperwork. After 30 years on the job, he had been an icon among those who had made Los Angeles a safer place to live. Only the best bosses get the helm at Metro, and Captain Lewallen was one of LA's finest. Yet on his last day, Captain Lewallen found himself still in uniform, a bulletproof vest underneath his blues, and his shiny pistol belt snugly around his waist. He had come to the office early, and there was a lot of work to be done—last day or not. His D Platoon was tasked with a "large" warrant in the Nickerson Gardens Housing Project in Southeast Area—a serious warrant targeting one of the most despotic gangs to murder and commit mayhem on the streets of Los Angeles—the Bounty Hunters. Most of the platoon had reached work by 6:00 A.M. There was some work to be done in the gym, some equipment to be checked out, and of course the tactical briefing.

There is usually a buzz at Metro HQ prior to a warrant—an unseen electricity that can be felt in the hallways, inside the cramped confines of the commander's office, and even in the snack room where officers down power bars and slam the vending machine for a Coke. Usually it's a positive vibe—a biochemical emission of anticipation. Today, however, the buzz was that of anxiety. There isn't an officer in SWAT who isn't intimate with the twists, turns, and dangers to be found in the Nickerson Gardens Projects. There isn't an officer who doesn't realize that any warrant served inside the Gardens has the potential for an explosive exchange of gunfire. Many of the officers in SWAT were baptized by gunfire in Southeast Area and remember being despatched to calls in the Gardens where their patrol cars would be shot at, they'd be ambushed, and sometimes even placed within the gunsights of snipers. "It's one of the few places in the city of Los Angeles where cops don't patrol in twos, but rather in fours."

The Gardens are bad, but the group targeted this warm autumn morning are real bad; "True s**t bags," claims one Southeast CRASH officer, "cruel, heartless, and f**king violent." The gang is known to commit drive-by shootings and then murder witnesses. They rob, steal, and peddle narcotics without being too concerned about the law. And anyone who attempted to resist them or cross their paths usually ends up with a dozen bullet holes in them. In the Nickerson Gardens, the Bounty Hunters are true terrorists. They take over an apartment belonging to a needy family and offer them a choice—either let "us" sell dope from here or we'll kill you! In many cases, they simply evict a family from a location and turn it into a drug supermarket. If the evicted family complains, they could get knee-capped (in a compassionate case) or simply blown away. The Bounty Hunters have become so notorious that their criminal enterprise is no longer just the obsession of the LAPD's Southeast Area CRASH squad, the LAPD's South Bureau Homicide Unit, and Narcotics, but the Los Angeles field office of the FBI has taken a serious interest in them as well.

When going after the Bounty Hunters, the SWAT officers understand that the warrant will be serious, it will be dangerous, and the possibility of gunfire is elevated along the SWAT "Richter Scale" of potential ballistic foreplay.

After an early morning workout and some additional phone calls to gather intelligence on the location, the briefing commences. One of the first in the room is the Southeast Area CRASH lieutenant who's overseeing the technicalities of the warrant and who's had to contend with the Bounty Hunters for far longer than he cares to remember. Dressed in a suit and tie covered by a royal blue LAPD windbreaker, the CRASH lieutenant smiles as he greets each SWAT officer entering the room. "Thanks guys," he says with a relieved smile on his face, "I appreciate your efforts." Slowly the room fills up with the SWAT officers, the SWAT commanders, and officers from Metro Division who'll be coming along for backup. Southeast CRASH is also represented for the warrant. They'll be attending to their business once the locations are entered and the suspects are secured and cuffed. There are several narcotics detectives present for the warrant as well—all muscle-bound and tough, with long hair in pony-tails and three-day's worth of stubble. The detectives carry with them legal folders with arrest warrants in them, and Remington 870 12-gauge shotguns, just in case.

Also present in the room, standing next to a film crew from the television series *LAPD*, are several members of the United States Naval Special Warfare community normally tasked with overseas hostage rescue. This unit, which doesn't officially exist, finds the LAPD SWAT tactics refreshing and innovative, and a source of mandatory study. Also present at roll call were additional officers from other Metropolitan Division platoons, plain-clothes narcotics detectives, and officers from Southeast Area CRASH. At the Nickerson Gardens, once the locations have been secured by SWAT, special agents from the local FBI field office will also come on the scene to begin their investigative field work.

After a brief roll call where attendance and non-tactical business are attended to, a SWAT sergeant begins the briefing by describing the five locations in the complex that are to be simultaneously hit. The responsibilities, tasks, and duties of each squad are described in detail at the briefing. One squad will handle apartments at the southeast corner and at the northern reach. Three other squads will be tasked with neutralizing three

A close-up portrait of a SWAT team debriefing following the successful execution of a high-risk warrant.

Sergeant Andy Lamprey, a senior SWAT sergeant and one of the country's most experienced tactical officers, looks on as his men assemble their gear, as he clutches his CAR-15 5.56mm assault rifle.

apartments in the south center area. Each apartment will be breached differently. One will have its front gates yanked off by a Suburban, one will have its front door taken off by a hydraulic Hearst tool (more commonly known as the "Jaws of Life"), another apartment will be handled by a battering ram and sledgehammer, and the final will have officers atop a ladder fire a Starflash device through a bathroom window and prevent the suspects from flushing the narcotics down the toilet once the fun and games have begun.

After the officers have suited up and grabbed their weapons, they drive their fleet of Suburbans to Central Area's roof-top parking garage where they will practice the mission one final time. Heavy-duty ropes are fas-

tened to the Suburbans to ready the vehicles for their "yank off" roles, and a "Fourth-of-July-like" display of the Starflash munitions is offered to the Southeast CRASH officers coming along. As the officers ready their gear and begin to banter about, Lieutenant Runyen engages Captain Lewallen in a brief discussion when his cell-phone rings. "It's on," Lieutenant Runyen shouts, "let's go—this one is hot and heavy!"

The officers fetch their belongings and head inside their vehicles for the convoy down the Harbor Freeway toward the confines of Southeast Area. As they near the location, worried about being discovered by ten-year-old lookouts armed with cell phones and beepers, they encounter a traffic snarl as a beer delivery truck blocks their route into the Gardens only a 100 yards from ground zero. After a threatening look from a SWAT officer carrying an MP5, the driver of the beer truck discovers it prudent to move immediately. Seconds later, the armada splits into five and the unit begins its work. The shouts of "POLICE—GET DOWN, SEARCH WARRANT" erupt through a relatively quiet morning in the Nickerson Gardens, as does the sound of cast-iron frames being tugged off their hinges, flash-bangs being tossed inside empty hallways, and Starflash rounds being fired through bathroom windows. The mission, with all five aspects happening simultaneously, looks chaotic. The officers move about all "SWATed" out, as suspects are brought to the ground and cuffed. There is a method to the madness and a choreography of order with everyone out there knowing exactly what he or she needs to be doing. The SWAT end of the warrant works like clockwork. Even the SEALs, on for a looksee, are impressed. "S**t, one claims, "we wouldn't have been up the ladder that fast, and we wouldn't have gotten the door off so quickly unless we used half a kilo of C-4. S**t these guys are good!"

The actual "hit" takes less than a few minutes. By the times the suspects and the narcotics are secured, most of the SWAT officers are debriefing their sergeants and Southeast CRASH officers, looking on anxiously. A small army of FBI agents have also descended on the locations, and begin to look over the evidence and to talk to the suspects. "I'm innocent," claims a 400-pound suspect handcuffed and laid out in a grassy front porch area, "the cocaine in the bathroom cupboard ain't mine," "Well," offers an FBI agent, "how'd you know it was in the bathroom?"

Firemen from the Los Angeles Fire Department are called in to handle a small fire caused by a flashbang, and Lieutenant Runyen and Captain Lewallen both want their officers out of there in a hurry. "These guys are incredible," claims a Southeast CRASH Sergeant. "They are in with a flash of glory and out like the wind."

In 1995, LAPD SWAT handled an impressive 51 warrants. In 1996, they will have handled in excess of 65. Back on the streets, in Rampart Area, the platoon is on patrol on a crime suppression detail. The addition of the platoon to a beleaguered patrol shift is of great support to a patrol captain faced with an ongoing crime wave. The SWAT officers change that equation immediately—their unmarked vehicles and distinctive black-and-whites are immediately noticed on the crime-paved streets of Rampart, as are the officers' bulging biceps, SWAT patches, and .45s holstered to their waists. There is a definite difference on the streets when SWAT is on patrol, a Newton sergeant once commented, "the knuckleheads [the bad guys] know that they are bigger, better, more experienced, and more dynamic than the average street cops, and they actually respect them. It's like coming to a touch football game with the Dallas Cowboys on your side. With these guys backing you up, you know you're gonna win."

The crime suppression detail in Rampart goes well. It's been a good week for the platoon. Some training, some work, and the warrant. Next week they are to host a visiting contingent from France's elite GIGN (Groupe d'Intervention Gendarmerie Nationale), the nationwide counter-terrorist and hostage-rescue force. Created on March 10, 1974, at a time when Carlos the Jackal and various other Palestinian groups were painting the streets of Paris red in blood, the GIGN is as experienced and as "elite" a force of operators as can be found anywhere in the world, yet coming to Los Angeles is a pilgrimage of sorts. Although they find it hard to accept that anyone on the planet is as good as they are, GIGN officers realize that Los Angeles is home to one of the finest units in the world and there is a lot to be learned from the officers of D Platoon.

Before heading out for the weekend, the officers check their gear, look at the roll call sheets and find out who is on call, and who isn't. Officers on call must be near a phone at all times, cannot go out drinking, and can, at the buzz of a pager, be summoned back to duty at a moment's notice. One never knows when SWAT will be needed, or when the officers of D Platoon will become that last line of defense keeping a situation gone bad from turning into a blood bath.

The unit is a mosaic of different races, cultures, ages, and background. Some are typical California-fare—blonde-hair, blue-eyed, surfer-types who look as if they could run a thirty-mile race without breaking a sweat. There are Latinos, African-Americans, Asian-Americans, and just about every other hyphenated American that can be found. Some have gray hair, a few wrinkles, and their biceps are adorned with tattoos. Some of the officers look as if they've only been out of high school a week. Their complexions, accents, personalities, and ages are as diverse as can be found anywhere in the United States, yet the unit enjoys a camaraderie evident in only the tightest of military formations. "SWAT is much more than a job," says an officer as he discovers he's on call, "it's a way of life!"

The unit has much to be proud of and, as its sergeants will always remind the officers, still much work to do. Yet in the 26 years the unit has formally been in existence, it has never lost a hostage. Few police units around the country, and around the world, can make that claim. Then again, none of those units are LAPD SWAT.

CHAPTER FOUR

CRASH
"Shootin' Newton" and the Gang-Bangers

It's nearing midnight on Pico Boulevard, and a hazy fall night has overtaken the confines of the area. Traffic is slow, but present. Along the thoroughfare, each block is marked by a beat-up old truck turned into a mobile taco stand by a family of recent arrivals from south of the border. A few homeless individuals, their shopping carts in tow, pick up bottles and cans and search the sidewalks for a scrap of spare food. The area radio has been slow this evening—a few assaults, one robbery, and an attempted burglary of a launderette. For Sergeant Paige, a 25-year veteran of the LAPD, the routine crimes are of little interest to him. As he hums a doo-wop song and scans the surrounding streets and boulevards, he is in search of only one thing—Gangstas." Sergeant Paige is a Blue-Knight nemesis to "gang-bangers," "homies," and any other slang word that can be thought of for a gang-member. He knows every gang that operates in the confines of the area. He can read and decipher their graffiti, and for this self-described hillbilly, he can talk-the-talk as well as walk-the-walk along with the best of them. He is a walking encyclopedia to a plague that has afflicted Los Angeles for the better half of this century.

As he makes a left on Central Avenue, gliding his unmarked Crown Victoria across the yellow reflection of a neon sign, the calm, yet pressing voice of an LAPD despatcher comes over the airwaves. "13-Crash-Twenty," she says, "reports of shots fired at Compton and 55th." "That's Bloodstone Villain territory," Sergeant Paige responds, "13-Crash-Twenty responding Code-3." Lights and sirens are sounded, the accelerator is floored, and some high-speed driving skills are employed to their maximum potential. "Sergeant Paige might have been on the job for 25 years," claims one of his officers, "but he has the

LEFT AND RIGHT: A sizable piece of evidence seized from the arrest at 41st and Avalon is cataloged and processed through the system by Officer Harrison.

77

Sergeant John Paige, center, responds to a 2-11 in progress in Rollin' 20s territory.

speed and reflexes of a 25-year-old." As Sergeant Paige reaches the location, he sees two LAFD ambulances already there, the chaos of human confusion, and shell-casings littering the street. Officers mill about, their Remington shotguns pumped and ready for service, while several detectives begin to canvas the crowd. A Ford sedan, ten 9mm holes through its rusting body, bore the brunt of the drive-by shooting. One man, an innocent bystander, took a round through his knee. Just another Saturday night in the "hood," claims one of the officers cringing as he thinks about how much paperwork this chaos will generate. "Just another night when the knuckleheads are out with their '9's," reflects Sergeant Paige. "Who

did this?" Sergeant Paige asks an eyewitness, who appears more angry than frightened. "What colors were the bangers wearing?" "Don't worry Cuz," the witness promises, "the shooters will pay." As the paramedics tend to the limbs pierced with high-velocity rounds and ready their patients for transports, the wounded offer hand-signals, cryptic gang-salutes, to the onlookers now crowding the sidewalks.

On the streets of Los Angeles, street gangs have become the source behind an astounding 70 percent of the city's crime statistics—from car thefts to homicides. Today, the "gangsta mentality" has become chic in many circles, and is popularized on MTV, in films, and by white-suburban wannabes who think it cool to call one another "G" and "Homey." But gangs have been an element of the Los Angeles geographic landscape for almost as long as Los Angeles has been a city. The first known street gangs appeared in the city in the early 1900s, in the Mexican neighborhoods. Mexican gangs sprang up as a neighborhood, or even block, self-protection force. The police department at the time did not patrol these outer fringes of the city, and the only way that the local residents could gain a sense of security and justice was through the young men who made sure that nothing bad went down in their turf. The gang members, known as the Pachuco warriors, later to be known as Zoot Suiters, would simply take care of their own. An outsider who walked into the neighborhood and caused trouble—from looking at a girl the wrong way to getting into a fight—usually ended up with a few busted ribs and a lesson in behavior. The gangs weren't truly criminal in nature, though they extorted money from local merchants and operated gambling and other vices for members of their communities. They were like a combination of cops, robbers, and neighborhood barons. The gangs adopted distinctive clothing and distinctive language, yet were not organized enough to be involved in citywide or nationwide criminal activities. Today, branches or "franchises" of the Crips and the Bloods can be found in over forty states.

Black gangs, too, have been in Los Angeles for nearly 100 years—the first "recorded" black street gangs being the "Goodlows," the "Kelleys," the "Magnificents," and the "Driver Brothers." Most of the gangs settled in and around the downtown area of Los Angeles, where most of the city's blacks lived in the 1920s and 1930s, and were very adolescent in nature. Although they were territorial, they were small, somewhat innocent, and never carried anything larger than baseball bats, chains, knives, and brass knuckles. A true turning-point in the history and evolution of the city's black gangs came about in the charred aftermath of the 1965 Watts riots, when blacks took up arms against the police in an ultra-violent display of rage and indignation. To many in the Los Angeles inner city, the Watts riot was a rite of pas-

"Yes Ma'am, Mrs. Gonzalez, your boy is a good child, but you see we arrested him with a .40 Glock and we need you to come down to the station house." CRASH officers are part cops and part diplomats.

sage. When the Black Panthers formed a few years later and grew into a strong presence in South Central Los Angeles, many of the young black gang members left the disorganized rabble of neighborhood gangs to grab a rifle or shotgun to become members. Others joined a similar Black Power group known as the United Slaves. The older kids and the politically savvy stayed in the movement, those who enjoyed busting heads and small-time criminal acts returned to their native gangs.

Rounds taken from a confiscated handgun—the gun might be clean, and it might have been used a day earlier in a 187!

One gang, made up of Fremont High School teenagers, often hung out around Washington High School. They were too young to be taken seriously by the Panthers, so they decided to form their own gang known as the Avenue Boys. The gang soon developed the nickname of "Baby Avenues" or "Avenue Cribs" and became known by the word "Crip." Crip gangs were established in several Los Angeles neighborhoods and in the city of Compton. The Crips, founded by Stanley "Tookie" Williams (now on death-row in San Quentin) were ambitious. They displayed a sense of loyalty and grand-city vision in regard to other gangs in the city, especially black ones. They were known by their blue shirts and blue bandannas, and were extremely violent. As the landscape of America changed into a violent land in turmoil, street gangs in Los Angeles evolved as well. Switchblades were replaced by revolvers. Baseball bats retired in favor of sawed-off shotguns. As the Crips expanded and moved into new territories, the body count rose. Los Angeles was witnessing a preview of its bloody future.

In the summer of 1972, a small civil war raged inside the Crip family of gangs—mainly between ele-ments from Los Angeles and their "bloods" in Compton. Since the Crips were strong-arming many of the smaller gangs into submission and oblivion, the remaining gangs opted to fight back. They changed their colors from blue to red, adopted the term "blood" as the name for their network of alliances and arrangements. The war and conflict over the Bloods and the Crips has been waged on the streets of Los Angeles ever since.

Gang warfare became a serious problem threatening the survival of the city the moment "rock," the Los Angeles term for crack cocaine, became a steady source of income and a gangland industry. Crack money bought new cars and heavy firepower. Its allure and addictive strengths swept like a hypnotic wave over the inner city. The Bloods and Crips, fighting over their shares of the market, began to wage turf wars for the lucrative narcotics market. In a sick sort of way, it was the "hood" version of corporate take-overs. Only these struggles were fought with AK-47s and Molotov cocktails, not lawyers and CPAs. It was chaos and the streets were riddled with bullet holes, the red blood of those shot, and the gold-colored brass of spent shell casings. Much of Los Angeles resembled a war zone. Adding to the violence were the hundreds of Hispanic gangs, also eager to enter into the narcotics industry, along with Vietnamese, Cambodian, Chinese, and even South American gangs.

One way that the LAPD sought to combat the plague was to form an elite unit within each area that would dedicate its manpower, resources, energies, and an above-board aggressiveness in fighting gangs. To wage a front-line war against gangs, whether it be a black Blood gang, a Chicano group, or even a Vietnamese gang working an extortion racket in the Valley, the Los Angeles Police Department created a special unit to be assigned to each area that would work solely with the community to fight the hoodlums—whether they were organized citywide, or controlled as little as two houses on a block. The phenomenon was known as Citizen Resources Against Street Hoodlums, though became famous by its

Paperwork—the scourge of police work. Here, an officer processes an arrest report for a member of the Krazy Kats, arrested for gun possession.

acronym of CRASH. There are CRASH units in each of the department's 18 areas, each combating a plague particular to a certain stretch of real estate.

The department's CRASH units became a national role model of how a modern police department could mobilize its resources. It's been a difficult fight, and one that shows no signs of letting up. In most areas of the city, fighting the gang problem is universal—aggressive street patrols, a well-documented database of intelligence, and the understanding that a good percentage of the crime in the area is, in one way or another, connected to the gang. In some areas, the gangs are the usual suspects of red and blue colors with a mixture of Chicano tossed in. In others, gang members could be speaking Mandarin, Korean, Vietnamese, or even Armenian. Each area has its own specialty. Newton Street Area has a little bit of everything. Newton CRASH, one of the busiest, is also one of the LAPD's finest.

The Newton Street Station house appears as if it's been standing almost as long as Los Angeles has been a city, and certainly as long as there have been gangs. One of the older sections of town, Newton Street Area covers a portion of the central area just south of downtown where the office buildings and Skid Row meet. The area is a lower-middle-class to poor residen-

A gun, seized in the waistband of a gang-banger, is run through the chain of evidence bureaucracy and ballistics testing.

tial area equally divided between black and Hispanic, though the area boasts many large businesses, factories, and industrial compounds. Many of the city's main thoroughfares, such as Florence Avenue, Slausen Avenue, and Pico, all run through the area. Of all the areas in the LAPD, Newton possesses a certain mystique, a certain sense of bravado, that exists nowhere else. Perhaps it is the fact that Newton is the LAPD's 13th Area, and "thirteen" can be construed as unlucky and unique in some circles. Its nickname has always been "Shootin Newton," less a descriptive comment of the area's marksmanship attributes than the fact that the area is always active, always busy, and always with the potential for violence. During the 1992 riots, for example, over 60 percent of the businesses in the area's confines were looted, then burned to the ground

Gang activity in the area isn't just intense, it is explosive. There are over 70 known gangs operating within the area confines—some have five members and are the baddest boys (and gals) in front of their house, while others control entire blocks, or even several streets. The streets, actually, resemble a civil warzone more than anything else. Among the more notable Crip gangs operating in Newton are the "40 Avalon Gangster Crips," "Southside 4 Trey," "4 Trey," "Eastside 4 Deuce," "Westside 4 Deuce," "5 Trey Avalon Gangster Crips," "5-Deuce Broadway Gangster Crips," "59 East Coast Crips," "6-Deuce East Coast Crips," "66 East Coast Crips," "68 East Coast Crips," and the "69 East Coast Crips."

In Newton Street Area, the Bloods aren't as powerful an equation as in other areas, but they are present, and are packing enough firepower and narcotics-fueled cash to wage the bloodiest of street wars. Blood gangs in Newton include "Rollin' 20s" (a.k.a. the "20's Outlaws"), "Rollin' 30s," "Rollin' 40s" (a.k.a. the "Bloodstone Pirus"), "5-Deuce Bloodstone Villains," "56 Bloodstone Villains," and the "Pueblo Bishops."

The majority of gangs in the area are Hispanic. Some have been working the streets of "Shootin Newton" for a quarter of a century, others set up shop once a rival group has been whacked in a drive-by shooting. Among the more prevalent Hispanic gangs in the area are the "Krazy Kats," "King Boulevard Stoners," "East Side Trece," the "Harpys," "Midnight Cruisers," "Locos Trece," "Loco Boys," "Street Saints," "Ghetto Boys," "Loco Park," "Street Villains," "Primera Flats," "Hang Out Boys," "Morgan Block," "Mid City Stoners," "Moonlight Cats," "Florencia," "Barrio Mojados," and the "Central City Criminals."

There are also a few Asian gangs, including the ultra-violent and "take-no-s**t-from-anyone" "LA Oriental Boys" that are very active within the area's confines.

Deciphering this small Bosnia of street turfs and attempting to keep a lid on a potentially explosive situation is the Newton CRASH team, led by 25-year-veteran of the force, Sergeant John Paige. With a warm smile that could disarm even the baddest gang-banger, Sergeant Paige has been a constant to the gang geographic landscape for long enough to spot a gang-banger 100 yards away. Most importantly, he has an ironed-will reputation on the streets that the gang-bangers respect and fear. "You don't f**k with the Sarge," advised one Rollin' 20s lookout to his young "Homey" protégé, as they were "tossed" on Central Avenue and 24th Street, "he's the man here."

What CRASH attempts to do, in its own unique way, is to constantly pressure the gangs so that the young thugs, at least for intermittent spurts, stay off the streets. When a CRASH car patrols a sector, anyone and everyone who looks like a gang-banger is stopped, talked to, and sometimes searched. "Gang-bangers don't walk these streets in three-piece suits and fedora hats," claims a CRASH officer with over three years of experience in his unit, "they wear colors—the typical 'gangsta' attire of bandannas, baggy pants, shoplifter jackets—and often tattoo their tags and gang names on various parts of their anatomy. We can pull up to one of these thugs, stop him and just by the 'King Boulevard Stoners' tattoo on his neck figure out, with a fair degree of certainty, that he isn't a stockbroker or a bus driver. They all have jackets (the LAPD slang for police records) a foot thick. And, of course,

the knuckleheads don't deny what they are. They can't. If you pull up to a Southside 4-Trey Crip gang-banger and say, 'Hey, who you banging with?' and they say, 'I ain't with a gang man,' and one of his buddies overhears him, his lack of testosterone in the face of the 5-0 (police) will result in, if he's a lucky SOB, getting the s**t kicked out of him. If he's unlucky, he could have bleach tossed in his eyes, he could wind up with a .38 slug through his knee—if he has also been suspected of stealing drugs or money, or sleeping with someone he wasn't supposed to, we'll eventually find his shot-up body in a dumpster."

Because the gang members commit so many crimes, and because there are so many of them within such a small area, the CRASH officers have developed a novel approach as to the cataloging and, for victims, identifying, the gang-bangers with something called a "Six-Pack." Gang members of similar size, shape, and color are photographed once inside the station house and then they are placed in manila-folder frames, six to a sheet. If a citizen has been shot at, robbed, or assaulted by a gang-banger, all that is needed is a simple description of the perpetrator.

Six-Packs are ideal photographic databases, and they constantly grow. "In a few years, we are going to need a warehouse just to store all the boxes with all the six packs displaying the ugly pusses of all the knuckleheads we've arrested," claims one CRASH P-III as he processes yet another gang member, this one a Blood, arrested with a .357 Magnum hidden in a denim jacket. The gun smells as if it has been fired recently—perhaps it was used to launch some rounds into the sky during a night of drinking, pot-smoking, and sex, or perhaps it was used for a point-blank execution for a body that will be found weeks later. The Blood is photographed, cataloged, and then processed through the system. He's been in jail before, and feels little fear to returning behind bars. In jail he'll be segregated with his colors and live in the gang members second society until a case against him can be built, or, more likely, a plea can be struck. California's penal system is beyond overloaded, espe-

ABOVE AND RIGHT: A mother-daughter team of crack vendors is arrested by Newton CRASH officers.

cially where juveniles are concerned, and anything that can be done will be done to keep a youthful offender out of jail.

The turn around in and out of jail provides the gang members with a sense of gang-color Teflon that, in their own convoluted psyche, makes them feel more invincible than they do anyway. "I don't give a f**k being in lock-up man," the Blood proudly proclaims. "I get three hots and a cot and I get to lift weights." Jail makes the gang-bangers colder and more reserved to the fact that they will eventually die, sooner than later, in some violent confrontation. It makes them dangerous to the cops on patrol.

Roll call for the regular Newton cops for the afternoon shift begins at 2:45 P.M. There is the summary of events, a briefing from the day tour, and the handing out of assignments. There were several homicides in the area since midnight, and the officers are given descriptions of the wanted suspects, as well as a small listing of their last known hangouts. The shooters are all gang-bangers, proud members of the 5-Deuce Broadway Gangsta Crips, and their work tools are 9mm semi-automatic weapons. One of the shooters is believed to be all of 14 years old, so the roll call sergeant warns his officers to display extra caution. "The big knuckleheads are heartless SOBs who'll shoot when they feel it safe, but the little monsters

A car stop yields great rewards and great dangers. Two CRASH officers search a vehicle for drugs, money, and weapons as its owners are cuffed and questioned.

know no fear. They'll rock'n'roll at the drop of a hat, so take no chances and assume that they are all strapped." Following the roll call, the officers will head to the armory and check out their Remington 12-gauge shotguns, prepare their vehicle, and begin an eight-hour tour on patrol. It is sunny in Newton Area, and a cool spring wind is felt coming in from the east.

CRASH turns out later than the rest of the cops, around 5:00 P.M., and mealtime is always taken first, when the sun is still out, because once the darkness emerges over the Newton landscape, CRASH gets busy—very busy! The unit turns out of a small and overly crowded office situated near the detective desks. The Newton Street station house is one of the few police stations in Los Angeles that looks like it

would fit right at home in New York City—the paint is peeling from the ceiling, leaking pipes hang overhead, and a pre-war (War of 1812, perhaps?) electric system makes the fluorescent lights occasionally flicker. The swivel chairs squeak and the office is a maze of file cabinets, paperwork, and office obstacles. By a desk to the rear of the rook sits a 400-pound gang-banger who calls himself "Goofy." Goofy's cohorts have chosen his name well, because Goofy is stupid. With a belly full of gang tattoos and arrested carrying a Beretta 9mm, Goofy is awaiting a chat with the homicide detectives concerning a "187," or homicide, that he has, quite stupidly, implicated himself in.

With the officers all present and the unit eager for an active Saturday night tour, Sergeant Paige

Gangstas are notoriously ingenious when it comes to hiding guns and drugs—especially a car used to transport large amounts of narcotics.

instructs his officers that the objective of the night's tour is bangers and guns. The gangsters don't mind a stint in the county lock-up or even time inside—it's a status symbol to them. But to many of the smaller gangs, losing a $500 automatic is a crimp in their style. Plus, besides having a gangster locked up for the concealed possession, there is one less gun on the street and one less finger to squeeze down on a trigger. On patrol, the 13-CRASH will not have to wait long until they make their sergeant happy. There are lots of guns on the street and lots of gang-bangers about to spend time behind bars.

Behind the wheel of his unmarked supervisor's Crown Vic, Sergeant Paige patrols the area—his eagle eyes in search of anything and everything that looks like, in his own words, "knucklehead trouble." The police radio is fairly silent, as is the citywide Tac-1 radio. An LAPD chopper, on patrol, flies overhead. It's still too early for them to make their almost nightly appearance over Newton Area in support of a patrol car or the CRASH unit, but it's virtually guaranteed that they'll be back in a few hours. Its twilight on a Saturday night, generally the busiest night of the week for drive-by's, gang killings, and other bits and pieces of thug mayhem.

As Sergeant Paige patrols down Central Avenue, the glistening lights of the downtown skyline appearing now with a majestic power off to the distance, a Code-3 call comes over the airwaves. A black-and-white patrol car has had its rear window shot out—the

Following a drive-by shooting between a Blood faction and a competing Hispanic gang, an officer shines his flashlight on the blood-soaked street in search of spent shells.

perpetrators, believed to be wannabe gang members, used a shotgun. Miraculously, none of the officers have been hurt. As the officers mingle about, in front of a Mexican-American grocery and the car awaits a crime-scene unit, two girls, no older than 14, come to the officers and complain that they have been sexually attacked by a male Hispanic, approximately 40 years of age, who exposed himself to them and fondled their behinds. The girls appear frightened and angry. Street justice will result in the perpetrator getting a slug in his groin, and the CRASH officers are eager to avoid any more paperwork this evening concerning a shooting. They split their patrol sectors up and search for the predator, seen with a white shirt and carrying a

bottle of beer, with tremendous zeal. Four blocks south, on a quiet residential street, a man fitting the description is found. The man appears startled by the cops, and cowers in fear. "Quietos, No se muevan," shouts one officer in Spanish, ordering the suspect not to move as cuffs are placed on his hands, "Like touching little girls do you?" another cop snickers. Inside the police car, the man begins to cry and look puzzled, not understanding why he is suddenly in the back of a police car. Sergeant Paige drives him to where the complainants are giving a statement for a face-to-face ID. "No, officer, that's not him," one of the girl says, "the guy who touched us was fatter." "Sorry sport," Sergeant Paige offers, "let me drive you

Gang graffiti in Newton Area—a memorial to slain comrades and a warning to others to stay away!

back to your home." Outside the now-no-longer-a-suspect's home, a small gathering of family and friends are yelling and screaming at the returning police officers. "We thought he was a bad guy harming children," Sergeant Paige says. "We are very sorry that we caused you or him any fear and we truly apologize."

One of the officers turns to Sergeant Paige and smiles, "It's a full moon out tonight Sarge, Lord knows what's going to happen."

What of course happens are a lot of gang arrests. Each time a CRASH patrol car finds a "knucklehead" and discovers a gun, drugs, or a wad of cash, they are brought in for questioning. Many times, they'll just be questioned, photographed, and then released.

As Sergeant Paige returns to the station house to file a report, the office is a busy and chaotic place. Several suspects, from a person suspected of stabbing his mother with a pair of hedge-clippers to a man the cops believe to be the Newton "butt-toucher," sit cuffed to a bench waiting to be processed. Inside the CRASH office, two officers fill out the paperwork on a Hispanic gang member, an angry SOB, who was collared carrying a concealed .38, a bag of pot, and over $3,000 in cash. "What the f**k you gonna to with my money, Homes," the gang member asks, "you take my money I's gonna blow your black ass away!" The officer, clearing the confiscated weapon for any rounds in the chamber, stares at the young punk with indigna-

Bullet holes in a sedan—part of the Newton Area landscape.

A drive-by victim is loaded into an awaiting ambulance for transport to a local hospital for trauma care.

tion, but then smiles to himself. "Threatening a police officer in front of about twenty witnesses," the tall muscular officer says quietly, "now there's a charge that should stick."

Because many of the gang members are under 18, CRASH officers must develop a certain skill in dealing with their parents and guardians. "Yes Ma'am, I know it's rough raising a teenager by yourself Mrs. Smith (a pseudonym) and I'm sure you are doing the best that you can," Sergeant Paige reassures a suspected gang-banger's mother, as he calls to request that she come in and pick her boy up, "but you gotta keep Jamal from hanging out with the bangers." Some parents are angry that their children are heading in such a dead-end direction. Many mothers, or grandmothers, come into the station house and beat the crap out of their charges. "You were carrying a what?" claims the father of an arrested youth caught carrying automatic in his sneaker as he slaps the back of his son's head with a ferocious blow. "Just wait till we get home!"

Sometimes, however, even mothers are gang members and employ their young children in the trade of the street. In one instance, near the corner of 41st and Avalon, in 4-Trey Gangster territory, CRASH units join in with an area-wide task force out to stop gang-related crack sales. A woman—the mother of several girls—dressed in her "blue uniform" is caught on her porch chopping up rocks of cocaine into small bags, while her children assist in selling the merchandise to passing-by motorists. The woman begins cursing wildly as the cops slap the cuffs around her wrists and a female searches her for weapons and additional narcotics. "I ain't be doing nothin wrong," the woman shouts, as rocks of crack and wads of money fall out of her pants pocket. "I wasn't selling no rock. I always say no to rock!" The officers smile to one another and then warn the woman to shut up. "You're caught red-handed, with drugs and money, and you are denying that you have anything to do with it? Next thing you are going to tell me is that you aren't a Crip?" "A Crip," the woman asks, "what that?" Inside the house, there

A .38 automatic is processed for evidence and its owner (former owner) questioned by detectives during a "slow" night in Newton CRASH.

are photos of the entire family, dressed in blue, displaying gang salutes, as well as photos of the individuals holding AK-47s and shotguns.

Outside the house, Captain Hale, the Newton Street Area commanding officer, talks to his officers on a job well done. A former pilot and boss with the Air Support Division, Captain Hale owns the chiseled physique of a flyer and the keen eyes of a street cop. "Good job people," Captain Hale tells the officers, as a female cop reads the Miranda warning to the arrested females; drugs and money off the street is always good news.

"The only way to stop the gangs, even for a little bit, is to make it so dangerous for them to do their s**t that they'll be forced to sit at home and watch cartoons," claims one CRASH officer as he wipes the sweat off his forehead following a foot pursuit. "Once they are off the street, they lose control of the hood, and once they lose control, they become less of a problem to the people who live here and are trying to get by."

Sometimes, the LAPD gets a little extra help in its war against the gangs from the federal government. On July 3, 1996, in a massive coordinated effort, Newton cops and FBI agents swooped down on the Central Avenue headquarters of the Bloodstone Villains, a particularly vicious gang that was preying on illegal immigrants. Twenty-one individuals were arrested in the raid, initiated by a SWAT dynamic entry. Dozens of guns were confiscated, and a large haul of drugs and cash was also seized. Several of the arrested individuals were booked on suspicion of attempted murder.

Back on the streets, with an hour or so to go in the shift, Sergeant Paige begins to reflect on his career fighting the gangs. In his 25 years on the job, he feels as if he's arrested the "same" people over and over. "It doesn't matter if a gangsta is arrested in 1972 or in 1992, they have the same stupidity, the same disregard for human life that they have always had, and probably always will." Moments later, two CRASH officers stop members of the Rollin' 20s, obvious gang-bangers, believed to be

The currency that drives any police unit is squad-room humor. Here, Sergeant Paige and his partner listen to a detective's humorous account of a knucklehead caught burglarizing a store, getting locked in, and then calling the cops to get him out.

selling crack from their beat-up Oldsmobile Cutlass. "Who you banging with?" asks Officer Melissa Quintana, as she runs one of the suspect's driver's license for a check. "Where's the guns and drugs?" Sergeant Paige, a seasoned veteran of how the gangs operate, frisks the male suspects and then lifts their blouses as he shines his flashlight on their flabby stomachs. He is in search of tattoos or scars from initiations. He finds what he is looking for. A few minutes later, two new smiling faces will be brought through the rear entrance of the station house. They'll be photographed,

processed, and arrested for outstanding warrants and narcotics and weapons possession.

A few moments later, as he passes the site of the under-construction Newton Street station house, Sergeant Paige responds to a call of a gang member fighting in the street. He is believed to be holding a Tech-9. "No matter how much the world changes around you," Sergeant Paige snickers as he announces a Code-3 response and begins to race down Central Avenue, "Newton Area and the knuckleheads will still be here!"

"Who you banging with, man?" "You strapped?" "You have the right to remain silent, anything you say. . ." A known gang member is arrested for illegal weapons possession.

After shots were fired at a patrol car, a Newton CRASH black-and-white responds Code-3.

Officer Melissa Quintana radios in information from a suspect's ID to check for outstanding warrants. The suspect looks on nervously.

CHAPTER FIVE

K-9 PLATOON AND AIR SUPPORT DIVISION
Support on Four Legs and in the Skies Above

It is just after 5:00 P.M. on a very warm autumn's night in the City of Angels, and the police radios, throughout the entire department, have been very quiet. Almost too quiet. Something has to give. Los Angeles is never this quiet.

Monitoring the city's band, Lieutenant Ron McColl, a towering figure of a cop with a befriending smile and a gleam in his eye indicating a lifetime's worth of police experience, sits in his office at Metro Division completing his paperwork before the evening shift commences. The office is crowded and activity around him is hurried, but Lieutenant McColl isn't frazzled. The early evening hours are always slow for him and his officers. Across the hall, however, in the office of D-Platoon's nerve center, the arrangements and coordination for a mega-warrant are being planned. SWAT officers, some carrying MP5s, race around the hallway, while others, running to the soda and snack machines, are storing up on sugar for a long night's work of planning and tactical preparation. In another room, several muscular officers wearing blue uniforms and camouflaged Kevlar vests return to the office following an equally hard

day at work. They are members of "B Platoon," the specialized anti-demonstration and VIP and Dignitary Protection element, and have just returned from Cal State University in Northridge where they stood on guard, in the epicenter of potential violence, during a much publicized debate between former Klu Klux Klan leader David Duke and an African-American civil-rights activist named Joe Hicks. Thousands of protesters, from all 360 degrees of the political spectrum, had gathered outside the lecture hall hoping to spark a fight and get their agenda on the Six o'clock News. "B Platoon" would have none of it, of course. Their mission is to prevent large-scale mayhem and violence and they provide deterrence by creating a blue line of law and order that few, in any, sane individuals would dare cross. The line of blue is supported by many of the cops carrying Remington 870 12-gauge shotguns, and a small cavalry of handsome steeds supporting mounted officers wielding night sticks and batons.

Although SWAT is the most famous and, some would say, most dynamic platoon in Metro Division, it's certainly not a lone wolf force. Metropolitan Division is the LAPD's elite, its special operations asset, that provides a high-powered and dynamic tactical solution to many problems, scenarios, and all-out chaos that the responding officers on patrol just

As observer Officer Theresa Harrell looks out the window of her Aérospatiale 350B during a routine patrol over Pacific Area.

Lieutenant McColl, the commander of the LAPD K-9 Platoon, conducts roll call at the LAPD Academy as his sergeants and officers look on.

cannot handle by themselves. Metropolitan Division's units consist of "A Platoon" (one lieutenant, one sergeant, and ten police officers) that handles the area's administrative functions and the ever-important armory. "B and C Platoons" (each deploying one lieutenant, five sergeants, and 50 police officers) that handle crime suppression details, VIP and dignitary protection, anti-riot and demonstration duties, and, when an area needs it, support patrol. "D Platoon," of course, is SWAT, and according to its official mandate, possesses the same tasks as "B" and "C" Platoons, only that it is also responsible

for handling barricaded suspects, high-risk warrants, extreme tactical scenarios, and hostage rescue. "E Platoon" is the department's Mounted Unit. Made up of former tactical officers within the area, the department's cops on horseback can, according to one veteran Metro Division, "disintegrate a riot into a peaceful dispersal in a matter of moments." Based at the eastern outreaches of the city, "E Platoon" is commanded by a lieutenant, and consists of three sergeants and 30 police officers. Their primary function is to work in the busy downtown area on crime suppression details to provide a four-legged tactical deterrence to any potential major and minor crimes being committed in the bustling business district. During a large-scale demonstration or the oncoming of a riot, "E Platoon" will work crowd control. "A demonstrator would have to be stupid to go against a horse," claims one Mounted Unit officer, "but knuckleheads are knuckleheads and some think that they can punch out a horse or even kick him. When man goes up against a LAPD horse," the officer adds with a smile, "man will always lose."

During riots, such as the 1992 riots that followed the Rodney King verdicts, *all* of Metropolitan Division, with the exception of "A Platoon" is mobilized into highly effective "Mobile Field Force" teams that can respond to critical situations forthwith, and with a tactical edge.

The final element of Metro Division is the K-9 Platoon—one of America's most experienced and tactically oriented K-9 units in existence. Commanded by a lieutenant, K-9 consists of four sergeants, and 16 officers (handlers) and dogs. The unit's primary function is to support the officers on patrol, in any and all of the city's 18 geographic areas, with searches for fleeing armed suspects. If there is a shooting, or if the suspect has been located in a building, or has taken hostages, SWAT is called in. K-9 has been a fixture of the Los Angeles landscape since the early 1980s, when the department finally came to the realization that dogs could be productive support assets to units on patrol. Because of the city's diverse geography, from urban sprawl downtown, to mountainous conditions in Hollywood and the Valley, patrol units required backup, basically an extra set of eyes and an extra set of legs (four to be exact) to assist in the pursuit of fleeing perpetrators. A man wanted for an armed robbery cutting his escape through the impassable woods of the Hollywood Hills might have the advantage when evading the cops, but a four-legged workhorse determined to seize its prey will not allow the difficult terrain to be a hindrance. The dogs will run up hills that would make a triathlete collapse, race through bush that would slice up uniforms and flesh, and not

demand overtime, a raise, or days off, no matter what the workload is. For Los Angeles, and its rising rate of crime, dogs provided an inexpensive, innovative, and effective solution.

Dogs had been used by the department for years, of course. Narcotics used drug, sniffing dogs on many of their warrants and searches, and the department's Bomb-Squad deployed dogs to sniff out explosives. But in a tactical sense, deploying dogs as a tactical search tool was something quite revolutionary and, many in the department realized, bound to be controversial, as well. Because suspects and other individuals were apt to be bit, departmental lawyers cringed at the potential lawsuits that could come their way. In fact, in the first few years of the unit's existence, approximately 350 individuals were bitten by dogs. While many K-9 naysayers attribute the individuals who had a "bite taken out of crime" as astounding, it was more reflective of the perpetrators not being familiar with the capabilities and authority of a pursuing police dog, rather than some deep-rooted departmental conspiracy aimed against a particular segment of the population. "Some of these knuckleheads," claims one Metro Division officer, "used to see the dog coming after them, and then try and fight, kick and wrestle with the dog. They didn't realize that the dog wasn't playing, nor was he some mangy junkyard animal meant to growl and deter. This dog was a figure of authority, and resistance usually resulted in teeth marks. And those who think of K-9 as inhumane to both the dogs and the felons need to remember that if an armed knucklehead resists arrest with a dog, he'll probably get bit. If that same armed knucklehead resists arrest with a human officer, he could get a lot worse." The end results are clear—when searching for a potentially heavily armed felon, having a dog on the beat adds the possibility of saving lives.

Although many opponents of the K-9 unit would have the public believe that there is a departmental agenda designed to unleash the animals out on a minority population in an uncontrolled campaign of

A team of handlers and their German shepherd demonstrate tactical firing positions while on a search for an armed suspect.

brutality, there are only two scenarios in which Los Angeles Police Department deploys its K-9 unit: (1) to search for a felony suspect, and (2) to search for an *armed* misdemeanor suspect. K-9 dogs do not walk a beat, are not employed to control apprehended suspects, and the unit never initiates its own searches. This two-pronged litmus test for deploying the dogs is sacrosanct in the department. "K-9 dogs will not be used to search for an unarmed kid found on the street smoking a joint," claims one of the officers, "nor will we ever use the dogs to assist patrol on routine jobs, such as domestic disputes and routine investigations. Our mission is very specific, very clear, and never mixed up." Soon, however, the K-9 Unit is hoping to expand its mandate with the incorporation of several search-and-rescue dogs. "With events like the bombing of the World Trade Center in New York City and the Federal Building in Oklahoma City," claims one Metro Division officer, "plus the fact that this city is earthquake prone, getting search-and-rescue dogs into the force is a sound idea."

Sergeant Don Yarnall, a veteran LAPD cop and world-renowned dog-trainer is in many ways the heart-and-soul of the unit. A trainer with the patience of Solomon and a professor's eye for his student's abilities, Sergeant Yarnall is one of the supervisors responsible for making sure that both handler and animal are ready for the dangerous task of searching for armed suspects. Although the unit turns out of its small office at Metro Division, the beginning of the day (usually one starting at 5:00 P.M.) starts at the LAPD Academy at Elysian Park where the supervisors, officers, and dogs all meet. Roll call is undertaken in an academy classroom, and after the unit's business is attended to, a daily training session commences on the grass in the center of the academy's running track. During the daily sessions, the officers wear protective "bite sleeves" and heavy-canvas "scratch suits" that are meant to limit the pain that the handler might suffer when his "puppy" becomes a bit too playful. Although the dogs are trained to bark when a suspect is found, and bite only when the suspect assumes the motion of flight and attempts to resist or flee, accidents can happen. The daily training is important, as is the work on the streets. Every three months, the dog must be re-certified through a series of obedience, search, and agility tests.

Not all dogs can become K-9 cops. In fact, the favored breeds for search work are German Shepherds, Belgian Malinois, and Hollandaise Herders. German Shepherds are favored because they possess above-average intelligence, have the endurance of a high-powered motor car (according to one British K-9 officer), and possess incredibly strong hind legs that enable them to jump very high. The Belgian Malinois, on the other hand, make terrific tactical dogs because they can run fast, even in the hot and humid weather of southern California, and are renowned for their hard biting abilities. Some of the dogs are donated by individuals who support the unit, others are purchased from breeders in the United States and in northwestern Europe. Sergeant Yarnall has traveled and trained with the Germans and Dutch, considered by many to be the world's finest police dog breeders and handlers. Most of the dogs, interestingly enough, are male—females tend to cost much more. There is an effort to ensure that the majority of the dogs in the unit are similar in temperament and appearance. All need to be similar in ability. Needless to say, Sergeant Yarnall and his staff scrutinize and screen each potential dog with tremendous care. The unit doesn't have the time nor the money to take on a dog that is borderline. Each animal needs to be a winner—one capable of eventually slinking through chain-link fences in hot pursuit of a heavily armed car-jacker.

By the nature of the intricacies involved in training a police dog, they are taught to obey only the commands of their handlers. They are taught to obey both voice and hand signals, and undergo the

A stoic portrait of an LAPD K-9 officer, gun (with flashlight attachment) at the ready, responding to a job in Wilshire Area.

When a call comes over the citywide Tac-1 radio requesting the services of K-9, the dogs and their handlers assume tactical command of the search and the inner perimeter. The unit handles two types of searches—outdoor pursuits (which are hot and heavy in adrenaline pumping action) and interior building searches (which are very dangerous, and as potentially explosive as anything in modern police work). Outdoor pursuits require the dog to rely on all his senses—sight, sound, and smell. The dog's olfactory senses are at least 150 times as strong as a human's and a well-trained dog can pick up a human scent in most weather conditions—especially if the individual being pursued is frightened and emitting a hormonal scent that only dogs can trail. On an outdoor search, a dog will usually race through bushes, trees, and up and down hills in search of the pursued individual; the dogs trail the scent with their nose and tend not to end their harried pursuit until the suspect is within range of their fangs.

Building searches are far more dangerous, because building interiors tend to be dark and a ballistic nightmare. There is an ever-present potential of officers firing at one another, or a perpetrator firing at the cops. During a building search, the responding area will always establish a safe perimeter around the suspected location—all bystanders and animals will be hurried away until K-9 arrives. The K-9 cops will usually get on a bullhorn and, in a strong English and Spanish pronouncement, warn whoever is inside that dogs are about to commence a search of the premises. Many perpetrators might not be scared of the "big bad police" but a Malinois with pearly-white teeth is another story. If there is no reply or "plea" begging to surrender, the dogs and the officers move in for the search. Tactical entry is always precarious. "Two officers, one handler, and one providing cover always fol-

routine list of obedience controls, such as sitting, heeling, and recall, before they are taught the art of K-9 pursuit. The K-9 unit is a unique beast in-as-much as both officer and handler have to be trained and be able to work and live together. They are a team more than the average two-officer partnership. The bond between a dog and his handler is similar to father and child. Police dogs live with their handlers, they become part of the officer's families, and are often cared for and fed better than the average family pet. When the animals are retired, usually at eight years old, they often become permanent members of the officer's family.

Suspects beware—when running away from the police, especially at night, there is a good chance that they will be coming after you in hot pursuit!

The K-9 patrol car—always on the scene every time patrol needs backup and support.

low the dogs in," claims a veteran K-9 cop recalling some hairy entries where known felons with guns were hiding out in a darkened abandoned warehouse. "The dog faces the greatest danger since he heads on hot and heavy after the scent of the bad guy; the handler, too, is at risk because his hands are on his firearm and his eyes follow the dog. The cover man, usually carrying his Benelli shotgun, has to secure both of them. It's dangerous work!"

Because of the treacherous aspect of their work, K-9 officers are a unique breed of cop—and perhaps among the most physically fit to be found in any department. Because of the strenuous nature of their work, the officers need to be fast and agile, and also need to possess the endurance of an Olympian; many of the dogs can sprint at an impressive 20-miles-per-hour, and the handlers need to be able to stay close behind. The officers deploy in full tactical kit—Kevlar body armor, Kevlar Fritz helmet, and Beretta or Smith and Wesson 9mm automatic. K-9 officers also carry the Benelli automatic shotguns. All their weapons are equipped with flashlight attachments. Because the K-9 officers are usually the first to come face-to-face with a wanted perpetrator, often one who is armed, they are among the most tactically skilled officers in the LAPD order of battle, second only, perhaps, to SWAT in their skill with firearms.

On one autumn night in Elysian Park, as a class of LAPD cadets raced across the track taking advantage of the cool night's breeze for several laps of hearty jogging, a K-9 officer was undergoing a difficult challenge—his certification as a handler. The certification examination is a rough one, supervised by the unit's lieutenant and sergeants, and a must-pass for any officer hoping to wear the coveted silver-metal "K-9" badge. The certification examination covers everything from how a handler is in control of his dog, to how he conducts the animal through outdoor and indoor searches.

Officer Tico, the officer undergoing the exam, is a bit anxious. In his "apprenticeship" with the unit, he has proven himself to be a top-rate cop and a top-notch dog handler. After the three-hour test that has taken the cops from Canoga Park to the Wilshire to Hollenbeck, both dog and handler pass with flying colors. The certification formally welcomes the proud officer into the unit, and although he has been through the thick of perpetrator searches and tactical assignments since coming on to K-9, the silver "K-9" badge is a rite of passage that cannot be taken away. After so much work and the anxiety of possibly not passing the certification process, many of the officers hope it will be a quiet night, so that a few cigars could be smoked and a peaceful meal had by all. The criminals, however, usually have other plans.

Minutes after receiving a hug from his wife and some slaps on the back from his fellow K-9 officers, Officer Tico finds himself heading toward the easternmost fringes of Hollenbeck Area, in the northeast corridor of the city. A man who has stolen a car has abandoned the vehicle in a driveway after being chased by police in a high-speed pursuit. The suspect is described as an African-American male, approximately 30 years old, and is believed to be carrying a gun. The pursuing officers conduct the search by-the-book: a chopper is called in to provide aerial surveillance and illumination; area officers, many cradling their shotguns, set up a perimeter; and everyone holds tight until the dogs arrive. It is dark, the area is

At around 4:00 A.M., after the successful search and apprehension of an armed car-jacker, a K-9 officer completes his paperwork before responding to the next job.

clustered with small homes, fences, and camouflaging foliage. An armed felon can be hiding in a million and one spots out of view from the chopper hovering up above. It is hard to hide from a small army of encroaching officers with their guns drawn—it is even harder when the saliva of a barking Malinois is spraying against your face.

Since their inception into the LAPD order of battle, four police dogs have been killed in the line of duty. While their loss has been a harsh price for their handlers to pay, the dogs did not leave behind any widows or orphaned children. Their sacrifice helped

save lives—both of the officers in pursuit, and of the sought-after felons, since a dog stopping a perpetrator, according to one Metro cop, "is a hell of lot more humane than a baton or a bullet."

Like K-9, the other LAPD unit that has, by far, become a national role model in terms of innovative support for patrol officers is the Air Support Division. The Air Support Division is the largest municipal police air component in the United States, and one of the largest in the world. In 1995 alone, the Air Support Division's fleet of 17 helicopters assisted in over 7,000 arrests. The unit responded to over 35,000 crimes in

At E Platoon's stables in the easternmost fringe of Los Angeles, a handler takes a police horse out for its morning exercise routine.

progress, over 1,000 vehicle pursuits, and 1,500 foot pursuits. These are incredible statistics and are a testament to the low-flying skills and sheer courage of the Air Support Division's aviators. According to one Rampart Area officer, who hopes to one day become an Air Support pilot, "Imagine where we'd be without ASTRO," as he gazes toward the sky at a Bell-206 Jet Ranger flying overhead. "We'd be left out on the streets vulnerable, lurking in the bushes with our asses exposed, and without our invaluable eyes in the sky. These pilots are like a third officer in every car, an extra pair of hands, and about 20 extra set of eyes!"

The LAPD's first deployed choppers in 1956 as a complement to its traffic division, to help monitor the

"E Platoon" horse transporters, always on call, and ready at a moment's notice to take the unit to the first sighting of any major disturbances.

soon-to-be-over-capacitated freeways and thruways. At the time, the department possessed only one chopper, a Hiller 12-C. Even in the innovative times of Chief Parker, the helicopter was never thought of as a tactical tool. Everything changed in the mid-1960s and early 1970s. Choppers first proved their abilities to tactically assist officers during the 1965 Watts Riots. In situations where many officers found themselves suddenly pinned down by rooftop sniper fire, police copters could check out rooftops and even side

Outside the academy, during a daily training session, a K-9 squad car awaits a call to action.

Sergeant Don Yarnall, one of the most experienced K-9 handlers in American law enforcement, briefs his unit of handlers prior to a night's work in the City of Angels.

On the rooftop tarmac at Piper Tech—the world's largest rooftop helicopter airport.

At the Piper Tech control tower, an LAPD Air Support Division officer checks in with LAX concerning an erratic low-flying aircraft heading toward downtown.

Before heading out toward their chopper, the flight board is always updated and corrected.

windows for any snipers or protruding gun barrels. Helicopter pilots risked the ricocheting bursts of rifle fire to help direct officers out of harm's way, and to safely direct officers into a targeted location. Before FLIR (Forward Looking Infra-Red), and before high-powered night vision devices, the department's confidence in the helicopter as a patrol platform was limited. Slowly, however, with the inclusion of high-powered field glasses and more stabilized aircraft, the unit began to take a full-time role in anti-crime work and aerial surveillance. Yet the aviation unit's true transformation into a support player came during the joint SWAT and FBI assault on SLA headquarters in South Central in 1971. The fire-fight was so hellatious and so much ammunition expended that choppers flew in supply missions bringing in more bullets and equipment to the under-fire officers.

Today, the Air Support Division is an integral element of law enforcement in Los Angeles and the department's fleet of 17 choppers have become as much a part of the city's landscape as Venice Beach and the Hollywood sign. At any given point in a day, 365 days a year, there are three LAPD birds in the skies over Los Angeles. There isn't a neighborhood in the city, from the luxurious streets of Brentwood to the desolate squalor of Rampart, where a night isn't interrupted by the whipping cadence of a helicopter's rotor blades coming in low, very low, and a powerful searchlight illuminating the darkened night with a blinding blast of fluorescent glow. The thumping beat of the rotors are heard most frequently in the worst neighborhoods of the city. There isn't an area of Los Angeles that isn't within ASTRO's reach and there isn't an area that does not call on Air Support at least *once* a day. During a routine shift, each helicopter often responds to an average of 15 to 20 jobs per two-to three-hour flight—a pretty remarkable statistic considering the fact that the choppers respond mainly to hot pursuits and jobs involving officers in need of assistance.

Air Support Division flyers "average" between 700 and 800 flight hours per year. "It would be impossible to police this city without helicopters any-

Officer Ed Provenzano, Air Support Division pilot, readies his gear before the commencement of yet another day at the office—500 feet high atop the city of Los Angeles.

more," claims a Newton sergeant responding to 2-11 robbery with lights and sirens flashing. "It just couldn't be done. We only have 8,000 cops in a city that is a bloated 465 square miles in size. The choppers are meant to become an equalizer of sorts, eyes and ears in the sky, that can come to our aid at a moment's notice, and be there in a matter of minutes."

The nerve center of the LAPD's aviation assets is the sprawling rooftop heliport at Piper Tech, just behind the Los Angeles River and Union Station. The facility is the world's largest rooftop heliport, making

Observer Officer Theresa Harrell stashes her gear inside a compartment as she prepares to undergo the pre-flight checklist with her copilot.

it a whirlybird adrenaline factory. Police choppers are constantly taking off and landing, and the control tower is constantly directing half a dozen small aircraft and choppers flying in and around the area. Yet for a department that relies so heavily on its aviation assets, Piper Tech is a calm and peaceful place to do police work. Though the pilots realize that in a matter of minutes they could be dead-center in the middle of a riot, or chasing a car-jacker who has just committed a cold-blooded murder, they attend to their duties with the utmost professionalism and cool. "There are dangers on patrol that we no longer face," claims one Air Support Division pilot, "and we face dangers and situations here that an officer riding in his patrol car can never imagine." One of the most dangerous periods in the history of the division came during the

An LAPD Air Support Division Bell 206 Jet Ranger prepares to take off in assistance of Rampart Area officers chasing a car-jacker.

With a small command module of flight instruments and law-enforcement gear, chopper pilot Ed Provenzano glides his bird in for a turn while patrolling over Newton Area confines.

1992 riots, when helicopter crews actually flew while sitting on bullet-proof vests and flak vests. It was chaotic and dangerous, and the threats to the police existed both on the ground and in the air. The burning businesses and buildings created a cloud of smoke which, when combined with the legendary notorious Los Angeles smog, made flying treacherous.

Becoming an Air Support Division pilot is among the most coveted postings in the entire department—ask just about any beat cop what he or she would like to do, and most will answer "ASTRO!" But the LAPD isn't interested solely in aviators, it wants cops, good cops, behind the throttles, and it requires that officers applying for the division have a minimum of five years on patrol logged on their belts. "Being a good cop is just as important as being a good flyer," claims one ten-year veteran of the division "You need to know, when pursuing of a vehicle or a suspect, just what might be going through his mind. A lot of this job is the robotics of flying and aeronautical mastery—a lot of it, though, is pure cop's instinct."

Before each crew heads out for a flight, meticulous maintenance is performed on each copter and the crews undergo a small litany of pre-flight checks with their machine and one another. The pilots and observers, appearing purely combat-ready in their green flight suits, polished-to-a-mirror's-reflection badge, and gold-metal wings, must know how to master a small arsenal of equipment once airborne. Inside the cockpit—beyond all the controls, knobs, and switches required to fly the aircraft—are gyrostabilized binoculars, a Nightsun searchlight, a P.A. system, a LoJack stolen-car homing device, and, of course, the device that turns night into day—the FLIR camera and monitor.

One of the most important pieces of equipment carried by the pilots and their observers is a special street atlas of Los Angeles, with all words in large type. Police instinct is important—some of these cops can navigate their way out of a Boyle Heights neighborhood blindfolded—but street names are of incredible importance when directing a small army of Code-3 cars to a crime scene. At 500 feet above the city, much of Los Angeles looks alike—two-story concrete buildings, parking lots, and roadways. Much of the geography is similar, bland, and identical to a patch of turf in another area.

The jobs these airborne cops receive are diverse, bizarre, pulse-pounding, and always hot and heavy. It is one of those days in Los Angeles when a trained ear could tell that the day would be a busy one. Following an unseasonably cold spell when crime, of course, slowed considerably because most of the bad guys stayed indoors, a heat wave of unseasonably warm weather drove the perpetrators right back out in the sun. Area radios were abuzz with reports of car-jackings, robberies, and assaults. The cold spell has pushed the fog off to the distance and visibility is pure, clean, and crystal-clear for a 360 degree radius. The Aérospatiale AS 350B flying on patrol is on a dual mission this afternoon, however. An LAPD photographer is on board, flying in the passenger seat, out to take some photographs of a home in Southwest Area that has been targeted for a warrant by a narcotics unit and SWAT. The photographs are needed by the SWAT officers so that a tactical plan can be formulated for the warrant, to be served three days later. The house is

photographed from every conceivable height and angle. The photo-reconnaissance takes a little over ten minutes, and by the time the photographer is returned to Piper Tech, there are multiple jobs coming over the radio requesting Air Support.

At an intersection in 77th Street Area, a team of two black males, one tall and the other short, used a sawed-off shotgun to car-jack a motorist at an intersection. While the victim was unharmed, one of the

perpetrators fired a warning shot into the air, leading the cops to consider the pair to be armed and dangerous. In the confines of the area, they ditched the 1995 Nissan Maxima near a junkyard and then continued racing away from the police on foot. "Air 14 en route," was the response that the observer, Officer Theresa Harrell, put out over the air. The cops in pursuit felt a sudden sense of security knowing that with a chopper en route, the suspects would not be elusive for long.

The Aérospatiale AS 350B was hovering over 77th Street Area in a matter of minutes.

As the chopper's pilot, Officer Edward Provenzano, glides the ship toward a low-latitude flight path, Officer Harrell grabs her field glasses and begins a play-by-play reconnaissance of the area, in constant radio communication with the officers below, while searching for the two suspects. To get up close and personal with their search, the chopper flies a dizzying orbit only 100 feet

LEFT AND ABOVE: Observer Officer Harrell is in search of the two elusive car-jackers, all the while maintaining radio communications with the officers 100 feet below.

With the help of the Air Support Division, two "alleged" car-jackers suddenly find themselves sprawled out on a 77th Street Area sidewalk awaiting a trip to the station house.

above the ground; the flight becomes tight and nauseating, but allows for an accurate surveillance of the area. The pilots have to beware of the elevated power lines, even a flying kite or a balloon—anything airborne can be a hazard to the safety of the ship and the crew. The crew also has to be on the lookout for a newscopter, monitoring a police scanner, that might be interested in transmitting a live-feed of the search for a local news update. While managing to fly tight and bank in sharp angles, both pilot and observer locate the two suspects with little difficulty—lurking behind a stripped truck at a corner junkyard. Their coordinates were radioed in to the officers down below and arrest was moments later. "Thanks guys," one of the 77th Street Area sergeants said as he gazed up above toward the departing Aérospatiale AS 350B. "Anytime Sarge," offered Officer Harrell, "that's what we're here for." As the suspects lay sprawled out on the ground, cuffed and ready for transport back to the station house, the chopper is already zooming at full speed to hover over a reported burglary of a residence in Hollywood Area.

On one job, over Canoga Park in the San Fernando Valley, officers from the area's vice unit were staking out a corner near a service station snaring motorists who had been soliciting the small army of invading prostitutes that had been turning residential thoroughfares into corner sex parlors. A female undercover, dressed in tight jeans and a revealing tube top, was standing on a corner "just minding her business" attracting men in search of a few moments of $10, $15, and $30 passion. One motorist, in a beat-up van, and apparently with five or six more bottles of Corona in him than he should have had, came up to the female officer, sensed a trap, and then sped off heading west at over 80 miles per hour. With the interlocking zigzag freeways and roadways that connect the area with the rest of the city, a suspect could have been

miles away by the time a concentrated search was raised. In Los Angeles, however, one click of the transmit button on a cop's Motorola radio, and ASTRO is en route. They are "old reliables" that can fly to a crime scene at 145 miles per hour—no matter what the traffic is like on the Harbor Freeway.

As patrol officers commence a pursuit and then search the area for any possible sighting of the van, a ship that was patrolling Pacific Area diverts its path northeast toward the units in need of aerial assistance. The patrol cars cannot find the van, but an ASTRO Bell 206B Jet Ranger, armed with FLIR, finds it in less than ten minutes. On a quiet street, the FLIR picks up a parked car emitting heat from its just-turned-off engine. The observer scans through his field glasses and confirms a hit. Patrol cars are directed toward the coordinates, and the van parked underneath a hanging tree is surrounded and apprehended.

At night, the City of Angels shimmers like a wave of sequins. It is an awesome view from the cockpit of a Aérposatiale as it races through the cloudless sky from job to job. The city's panorama of mountains, neon, and moving brake lights is dazzling and sometimes appears far too peaceful. The pilots cannot let their minds wander or let their concentration be diminished even for a second.

There is a car chase over the 405 Freeway, and the stolen car is racing about at speeds in excess of 100 miles per hour. By the time the chopper reaches the chase, the suspects have crashed the car and run off into a wooded area, covered by trees, gullies, and thick underbrush. As the chopper illuminates the search with its Nightsun power lamp with a thirty-million-candlepower-strong beam of light, three K-9 vehicles announce that they, too, are responding Code-3.

Few cities have such an effective tandem in their specialized units as the Los Angeles Police Department. "If we don't get you on four legs and bite you on the ass, we'll certainly get you from 100 feet up," claims one Wilshire officer who has been able to arrest hundreds of felony suspects with the help of his "four-legged and airborne backup."

113

CHAPTER SIX

SOUTH BUREAU HOMICIDE
"187" Los Angeles

It is a top-ten list that no city wants to be on. Being among the top ten in the homicide category does not get a city any extra prestige, fame, or tourist dollars. On the contrary, this list brings a sense of fear and foreboding to a metropolis, and images of streets littered with corpses and paved in blood. For yet another year, according to the FBI, Los Angeles ranked nationally in the top ten of cities with the highest per capita murder rates. To many of the city's residents, the news only reinforces their sense of fear about living in a city where crime seems to know no bounds and limits. For city leaders, the news is a mark of blood-red ink against the efforts of the LAPD and the criminal justice system to check crime and make the city a safer place to live. To the detectives who work homicide for the LAPD, the news is not even worth a second look. They don't need statistics to tell them about the skyrocketing murder rate. Their profession is to solve the puzzle left after the body count has been taken. If the streets are paved in blood, then it is their unforgiving task to wade through the debris and find a killer.

Per capita statistics mean even less to Lieutenant John Dunkin, the commanding officer of South Bureau Homicide, one of the city's finest (and busiest) homicide unit commanders. Nor does Lieutenant Dunkin need any news from the FBI—if he needs the Feds to help out, he just has to walk down the hall and speak to a G-man. The Los Angeles Police Department divides its 18 territorial areas into four separate bureaus, each mini-commands where task forces of detectives and officers become a clearing-house for the crime committed in each distinctive patrol area. Central Bureau consists of Central, Rampart, Hollenbeck, Northeast, and Newton Areas. West Bureau consists of Hollywood, Wilshire, West Los Angeles, and Pacific Areas. Valley Bureau includes Van Nuys, West Valley, North Hollywood, Foothill, and Devonshire. Finally, South Bureau consists of some of the city's most crime-ridden areas—Southwest, Harbor, Southeast, and 77th Street Areas. South Bureau is, per size and capita, the most congested bureau in the city. With a population of nearly 630,000 documented residents (and at least half as many undocumented) crammed into an area of 58 square miles, combined with the poverty and gang activity in South Central Los Angeles, there is little wonder why South Bureau leads the city in murders. In 1995, 269 individuals were murdered in South Bureau; 77th Street, with 82, and Southeast, with 90, were in close competition with

Detective Brent Josephson, one of South Bureau's finest homicide sleuths, catches a case.

Lieutenant John Dunkin (right) confers with one of his most senior detectives following a gang- and narcotics-related slaying in South Central.

race against the clock, in a race against the legal system, in a race against the dwindling memories of witnesses, and in a race against their ever-larger workload. Most detectives in the bureau will handle approximately 15 cases a year—far too many by most police standards. Many patrol officers, hoping to be detectives, find the case-solving aspect of the job fascinating and glamorous. But there is nothing glamorous about being paged at 4:00 A.M. to look through a crime scene where a young boy, guilty of nothing more than wearing the wrong color or looking the wrong way, had most of his head blown off by a 12-gauge shotgun fired point blank behind his ear. It is tedious, bloody, nauseating, heart-wrenching, and, in trying to put killers behind bars, perhaps the most important aspect of modern police work today.

From its outside appearance, the South Bureau command center looks too neat, too sterile almost, to be a police department nerve center. Located on the ground floor of a mall on Crenshaw Boulevard, the neatly carpeted office building is a camouflage for the gritty work that goes on in the station nearly

one another for the bureau championship. It is a dangerous place to work.

Lieutenant Dunkin is a hands-on commander of what many consider to be the department's finest squad, however. The former paratrooper and OIC of the LAPD Press Relations Office, Lieutenant Dunkin is a sophisticated and smooth commanding officer who realizes that his detectives are often facing an uphill battle to solve a murder. Whether it's a crime of passion or a gang-related drive-by in which an innocent bystander has been struck in the head by a Black Talon bullet, the detectives will find themselves in a

Patrol officers, SID technicians, and an LAPD photographer look on as evidence is tagged, numbered, and photographed.

24 hours a day. The entire spectrum of humanity is represented in the caseload in that office—human perversion, aversion to responsibility, human cruelty, and sadness. There are homicides resulting from burglaries gone bad, child abuse instances where young children have been savagely beaten or tortured, domestic disputes, gang-related activities, narcotics deals gone sour, robberies, rapes, and other tidbits of chaos. There are gunshots that have killed the bureau's victims, knife wounds, and the brute force of fists carrying blunt objects being thrust upon the human skull. Victims are men and women, the guilty and the innocent, under 18 and over 65. In South Bureau one can find victims in the port of San Pedro, in Harbor Area, where a coke deal gone sour has resulted in a person receiving a gunshot wound to the heart, and in the infamous Nickerson Gardens, where boredom, apathy, and gang-induced savagery has reduced "187," the California Penal Code term for homicide, to just another thing that happens in the neighborhood.

"South Bureau Homicide, Detective Josephson, how can I help you?" In the squad room, the telephone appears to never stop ringing. Detectives are usually out of the office, either responding to a fresh homicide, or following leads and investigating dead-ends in old cases. The detectives wear conservative suits, carry their Smith and Wesson or Beretta automatics in polished leather shoulder holsters, and brace themselves for every time there is a shooting and the possibility of a victim dying. Unlike a patrol squad room, there is little time for banter, and even fewer opportunities for gossip. "Detectives are egos with nice suits and zealous work habits," claims one detective supervisor. They are individuals who work best alone or in the expanded team of two. Each team of two detectives has its own method working a case, its own idiosyncrasies, and its own success rate. There are some teams that are brilliant case-closers that the entire bureau respects (or is jealous of). There are teams of dedicated professionals, and there are teams of less enthusiastic individuals who do not possess

Perhaps just an abandoned watch, or an invaluable clue, every piece of evidence in a crime scene is considered crucial until discounted later.

long and illustrious careers in the unit. The most important aspect of the work is not to let the case get to you. While it is impossible not to be affected by the carnage and senseless loss of life, the detective has to detach himself from the emotions of the crime and concentrate his energies on the facts, the evidence, a lot of research, the grinding of shoe leather, and the ever present factor of luck. As a personnel manager, Lieutenant Dunkin's squad is a mixture of brilliance, energy, street-smarts, and tired cops. Each detective likes to work differently, and enjoys a different aspect of the job. Some are masters at canvassing a neighborhood, knocking on doors, and getting out there with the public. Others enjoy the investigative aspects of the job, where they sift through suspect jackets (police files) and comb through ballistic evidence. "The pairing of the detectives," Lieutenant Dunkin admits, "is perhaps the most important decision of a

An SID investigator takes a ground measurement of where a shell casing has been found and where the victim's body was. The victim's bloody clothing is still on the scene.

homicide lieutenant. How that team works, how their personalities mesh, and how good a judge of character you are will reflect on how those two detectives work together."

Human nature plays a great role in perpetrating the act of homicide, and it has a lot to do with how the crimes are solved. While there are cases that naturally eat at the hearts of many of the detectives, the command is a political beast as well, and Lieutenant Dunkin is often forced to shift resources to cases that strike a chord with the public and receive extensive media attention. Only one-third of all murders in the city even make it to a brief one-inch mention in the Los Angeles Times. "We like to treat each homicide as if it were equal, from the killing of a media sensation to the murder of an anonymous soul, but in reality the more high-profile the case," admits Lieutenant Dunkin, "the more assets we need to invest in bringing it to a close. It will mean that we pull detectives off of existing investigations in the hope to solve this one."

One particular case was the February 22, 1995, shooting of schoolteacher Alfredo Perez, shot in the head as he taught his class at the Figueroa Street Elementary School. It was as random an act of violence as could exist—an innocent teacher shot as he taught a class of kids. South Bureau Homicide was called in because it was initially believed that Mr. Perez would not survive his injuries, and a homicide investigation began. Detectives knew it was a gang-related shooting, and knew that gang violence often causes any potential witnesses to suffer sudden cases of memory loss. But because the shooting sparked intense local media pressure (even getting attention from President Bill Clinton), Lieutenant Dunkin was under pressure to solve the case. A short while later, two gang members were arrested. The shooting was indeed a drive-by, but it wasn't a revenge shooting, or anything related to a drug deal gone sour. The shooter, alleged to be a gang-banger named "Slim," had fired the three shots on a dare from another gang-banger, one named "Mont Duce." It was as senseless as a shooting could be, but all too familiar ground to cover for the bureau's homicide cops.

For other cases, there is great emotional pressure to bring the killer to justice—especially in cases involving small children. One such case was the rape and murder of 12-year-old Monique Arroyo, killed "allegedly" by her 44-year-old uncle, Eloy Loy. Loy was a classic suspect. "He had," according to one of the detectives, "all the classic profiles of someone who could have perpetrated the rape and murder—history, inclination, and opportunity." Loy was a paroled sex offender who had served 14 years in the State Penitentiary in Tehachapi for the rape of an adult. He spent time in the house with the victim, and he had access and opportunity to assault her, abduct her, and murder her. The case of an innocent girl assaulted, kidnapped, raped, and murdered tugged at the hearts of many of the detectives. Many have children of their own, and Lieutenant Dunkin's detectives were adamant about putting the killer away.

Initially, Loy was arrested on parole violation on a separate charge. When DNA evidence returned from the lab implicating Loy beyond a reasonable doubt, he was charged with the killing.

In a homicide investigation, it is crucial that the crime be solved in the first week to 14 days. Otherwise, physical evidence gets weaker, witnesses become few and far between, and the chances of ever solving the case become slimmer. When a shooting occurs and it appears as if the victim is in bad enough condition that he might die, South Bureau Homicide

The bloody remains of a gang-related violence—the results of four 9mm shots to the midsection.

gets the call. Usually, there is a team that "catches" cases. The phone rings, they answer it, and then race out to a crime scene to observe the body(ies), begin canvassing the area, and start the preliminary paperwork. "You can work a hundred murders," claims one homicide detective, "and no two are the same."

If the hardened detectives are shocked by anything, it is the brutality of many of the murders and the young age of the perpetrators. Many victims are no longer *just* shot. They are savagely tortured, some have Drano shoved down their throats or cigarettes burned into the genitals and eyeballs. Sometimes, as a calling card, the killer will even carve his initials into the flesh of a victim. And then, when any sense of suffering is no longer there for the enjoyment of the murderers, a gun is simply placed to the forehead and the trigger squeezed. The killers in many cases are so cruel that even the cops fear them. The killers are also so young that the detectives simply write off the generation as lost. "These kids are stone-cold killers,"

119

As the lead detective talks over a case with the coroner's office, an LAPD crime-response unit responds to the homicide scene. On certain streets in South Bureau, these trucks are seen more often than mail trucks.

claims Lieutenant Dunkin, unable to contemplate, at least with any reason, how an 11- or 12-year-old can take a gun and simply kill another human being. "Where are their souls? Their consciences? They have none. They are creatures capable of killing on a whim and without thinking twice about it."

One case in point that rocked Los Angeles was the brutal murder of 83-year-old grandmother Viola McClain, killed on her porch across the street from the Nickerson Gardens project on 111th Street. In the hours before Mrs. McClain was murdered, a group of kids and an adult brutally gang-raped a young girl in an abandoned house, and then tried to set fire to the building, with the girl still alive inside. When the rapists began to set fire to a mattress outside the abandoned building, Dumar Starks, Mrs. McClain's 33-year-old grandson, came out of his house and began to confront the group. He was threatened with a firearm, and quickly went into his house to grab his own weapon. When Mrs. McClain emerged from the house to see what was going on, she was shot through the neck as she stood on her porch. The murderer, remarkably, was a 12-year-old who showed no remorse for either the rape or the murder. His mother, unremarkably, couldn't believe that her baby boy could be the perpetrator.

When investigating gang-related homicides, the detectives come up against dozens of roadblocks that hamper their investigations. Many times, when detectives are searching for a known gang-banger and stop by the suspect's house, they will find the wanted individual coming from a single-parent home, with either his mother or grandmother being the soul adult in his life. "Did you know Tookie was banging?" asks one detective to a 33-year-old mother of an 18-year-old wanted for a cold-blooded homicide. "No way, that's bullshit," the mother claims. "Tookie is a good boy and he takes care of his own." The house, a wreck of a small one-story home, is spartanly decorated, though framed photographs of Tookie and his gangsta friends sits proudly over the mantle. In the photos, Tookie is with his Homies, in colors, displaying gang-salutes and holding an AK-47. In a few of the photos, Tookie's mom is also in gangsta pose, saluting, and clutching a malt liquor bottle. In one photo, Tookie's mom is even seen holding a shotgun.

Finding witnesses willing to cooperate in a gang-banger slaying is also next to impossible. If a gang even suspects that a witness has talked to the police, the witness's entire family is at risk—at best, their house will be firebombed; at worst, the victim of a point-blank shooting. In the Viola McClain case, for example, South Bureau Homicide had to relocate over a dozen witnesses against the gang involved.

The gang violence in South Bureau has become so bad that the FBI has opened an office right across the hallway to assist the detectives in their war against the gangs. The task force is known as C.O.M.I.T. (Cooperative Murder Investigation Task Force). When the homicide detectives need help closing down a murderous gang, the Feds often go after that criminal enterprise with federal anti-racketeering statutes that guarantee a trip to a hard-core federal facility for a very long time.

Once a murder has been committed and the detectives, usually two per homicide, are deployed, witnesses and evidence are gathered. When witnesses are interviewed, they are always separated, thus keep-

Detectives and patrol officers confer on the killing. Patrol officers can provide a ton of information about a crime scene, and even about a victim. In this case, the officers had known that the victim was into narcotics and a known members of the Crips.

ing their stories sincere. When suspects are interviewed, however, the detectives become master showmen trying to get at the truth through guile, smarts, and old classic detective tradecraft. "There are pairs who employ the good cop/bad cop routine," claims one detective, "there are those who try and become pals with the suspects, and there are those who use mental games. These knuckleheads are not brain surgeons. Present them with a series of choices, and they usually lie alot, but then fold."

There are some detectives, Lieutenant Dunkin admits, that are simply made for this type of work, and are great teams. Others are less capable. Some,

over the course of time, have simply been burned out by all the bloodshed and killing. They have lost their zeal, their motivation, and their competitive edge. They begin to close fewer and fewer cases, and care little about if the perpetrators get caught or are on the streets to kill again. "In these cases," Lieutenant Dunkin adds, "I usually suggest that they transfer somewhere else where the pressure won't be so great. Sometimes, the burn-out doesn't happen, but it usually begins to surface after 15 years. Once they stop caring, if not for the victims then for their closure percentage," one detective adds, "then it's time to go." "After all," the 20 veter-

ABOVE AND LEFT: Marijuana and cocaine paraphernalia were found in the victim's house. Also uncovered were half a dozen pit bull terriers, three shotguns, and thousands of dollars in cash.

an adds, "we detectives might be many things, but we are all egos with feet!"

It is a warm summer's night in 77th Street Area, and a 17-year-old, for no apparent reason, ended up dead on a street corner near 54th Street with a .45 slug to his head. It was a grizzly sight. Head wounds are known as bleeders, and the area surrounding the victim's body was awash in his blood. Patrol officers secured the sanctity of the crime scene, trying to find the first batch of witnesses, and any bits of physical evidence that would be visible under the orange glow of a street light and the glow of a Mag-lite flashlight. There are no shell casings found, and the dozens of people who were on the street that evening simply lost all access to their memory banks. "Nobody saw

nothing," one of the detectives remarks to a patrol supervisor he knows. "What else is new!"

The morgue truck is brought in, as is a van from SID, the Scientific Investigative Division, that will collect all evidence from the crime scene. A police photographer begins to take pictures of the corpse and the crime scene, as well. "I don't want the family to see him like this," shouts one of the detectives to a patrol officer who was about to head to the victim's grandmother's house to bring her to the scene to ID the body. As the grandmother was driven the few blocks to see her grandson for the last time, the detectives and the technicians from SID carefully wrapped a towel around the victim's forehead, carefully camouflaging the gaping head wound. "The woman's

123

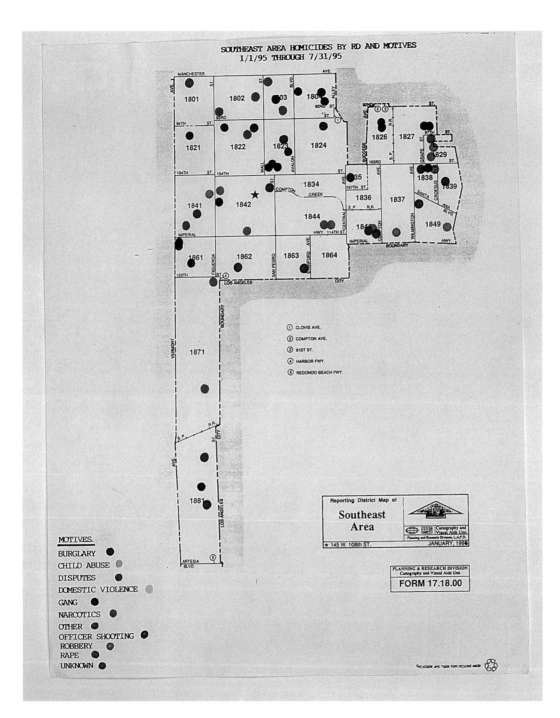

SOUTHEAST AREA HOMICIDES BY RD AND MOTIVES
1/1/95 THROUGH 7/31/95

① CLOVIS AVE.
② COMPTON AVE.
③ 91ST ST.
④ HARBOR FWY.
⑤ REDONDO BEACH FWY.

Reporting District Map of
Southeast Area
Canography and Visual Aids Unit
Planning and Research Division, L.A.P.D.
★ 145 W. 108th ST.
JANUARY, 1995

PLANNING & RESEARCH DIVISION
Canography and Visual Aids Unit
FORM 17.18.00

MOTIVES
BURGLARY
CHILD ABUSE
DISPUTES
DOMESTIC VIOLENCE
GANG
NARCOTICS
OTHER
OFFICER SHOOTING
ROBBERY
RAPE
UNKNOWN

124

The map board in the South Bureau Homicide squad room—the map is color coated to indicate gang territory.

A plain-clothes homicide investigator grabs his Remington 870 shotgun prior to embarking on a warrant with SWAT to catch a 187 suspect.

gonna be traumatized enough by the sight of her dead grandson," claimed the detective to a sergeant assisting in the investigation, "I don't want her to have to suffer any more than need be."

Back at South Bureau Homicide, Lieutenant Dunkin sifts through the mountain of paperwork that the supervisor of a 60-man detective force must endure on a daily basis. As he reads through reports and investigation updates, one of his

An example of a Area murder flow chart and map—used by the bureau to track and monitor homcides. *Courtesy: LAPD*

The South Bureau Homicide mission statement—hung prominently at the entrance to the squad room.

ing the guilty to justice, and the resources that the department is willing to invest in solving cases, are enormous.

Back in the office, it is a Wednesday afternoon and the day shift is about to pack their bags and head home for the day. A Southwest Officer enters the room to drop off a packet of material to a detective investigating a double-homicide. Looking at the "suits," the computers, and the confident eyes each detectives carries with him like a second gun, the police officers say to another detective in the room, "Gee, I'd give anything to get off patrol and be a detective." The officer, a boot (as rookies are known), will

With a suspect's "jacket" in his hands, Detective Brent Josephson enters the "box," the interview room, to talk to a 187 suspect.

younger detectives knocks on the door and requests permission to have Air Support fly him down to Scottsdale, Arizona, to pick up a witness. The witness, a flaky crack-addict who has no ID and, therefore, would not be allowed to board a commercial flight, was an eyeball witness to the murder of an alleged drug dealer. The murder did not spark front-page headlines, and the media never even bothered to print the name of the victim or the circumstances behind his bullet-riddled death. Nevertheless, for the LAPD and South Bureau Homicide, it is a case and it needs to be solved. LAPD detectives might have been publicly maligned in the "Trial of the Century" of the O.J. Simpson case, but their determination in bring-

The LAPD detective's badge.

Lieutenant John Dunkin (right) hears the "hunch-view" of the homicide from two of his most-seasoned investigators, in front of a "187 crime scene."

On scene where a man was shot four times with a 9mm automatic, Lieutenant John Dunkin and his team confer on strategy and possible leads, as a SID investigator assembles and tags physical evidence.

need to be in uniform, on the streets for a minimum of three-and-a-half years before being allowed to take the civil service examination where he'd qualify for a detective's badge. Yet the detective, eyes red and working on a second marriage and third ulcer, stares at the officer's naiveté and eager ambition and is in no mood to go over the bureaucracy involved in becoming a detective. "It's not like on TV kid, it's not all glamour," the detective begins to lecture in a low-key voice, but his speech is cut short by the phone ringing. "Hello, South Bureau Homicide? A shooting where? How many victims? We'll be right there!"

INDEX